KILLER CHILI

Library of Congress Control Number: 2007935877

ISBN-13: 978-1-60380-005-1

Cover photograph: Jupiterimages

Killer Chili: Savory Recipes from North America's Favorite Restaurants is produced by becker&mayer!, Bellevue, Washington.

www.beckermayer.com

Design: Kasey Free

Editorial: Kate Perry

Image Coordination: Stephanie Anderson and Lisa Metzger

Production Coordination: Shirley Woo

10 9 8 7 6 5 4 3 2 1

Manufactured in China.

Chronicle Books LLC

680 Second Street

San Francisco, California 94105

www.chroniclebooks.com

KILLER

STEPHANIE ANDERSON

CHILI

Savory Recipes from North America's Favorite Restaurants

CONTENTS

Canada

INTRODUCTION

One of the best things about chili—besides the delicious, mouthwatering flavors—is its versatility and adaptability; playing with the spices and cooking techniques in each recipe is at the very heart of making chili. Even if two chili recipes match on paper, the ingredients usually end up a tad "adjusted" by the time the concoction reaches the bowl. The makings vary from one enthusiast to another, and from region to region, and with as many different ingredients as you can use in chili comes as many (or more) opinions about what makes the "best" chili. Creators of Texas-style chili, for instance, firmly and unequivocally eschew beans and any vegetables (except chile peppers, of course); Cincinnati chili more closely resembles an Italian bolognese sauce; both East Coast and Midwestern chili tends to be a bit sweet and contains beans, meat, and tomatoes.

Self-proclaimed chiliheads go to great lengths to prove they know all there is about chili. H. Allen Smith,

a prolific author considered by many to be the official chili oracle, claimed in his aptly titled manifesto "Nobody Knows More About Chili Than I Do," published in *Holiday* magazine in 1967, that he and his brother did not speak for more than a year after a falling-out over their antithetical views on chili making. Smith also wrote that had he known about Lyndon Johnson's opinions on chili, he would not have voted for him in 1964. I doubt very much that tomato soup ever inspired anything close to that.

While different varieties of chili are made all over the world, the fare is inextricably linked to the culture and history of the Lone Star State; in fact, it's the official state dish. Devotees widely believe that chili was invented in Texas, perhaps due to its proximity to Mexico. Texas saw the very first chili parlors, small, family-owned joints that whipped up and served nothing but Texas-style bowls of chili, dubbed "chili con carne." The competitive spirit surrounding chili was

likely born in these establishments, as each one had its own closely guarded secret recipe.

Due to the chili craze in Texas, chili parlors opened up in many corners of the United States (and some even in Canada), but most of these ventures have since closed. The ones that do still exist, however, maintain an essential secrecy around their recipes. Take Cincinnati, Ohio, for example. Cincinnati-style chili is a far cry from the Texan variety, but Ohioans are just as fanatical. This type of chili was reportedly invented by Greek immigrants, and is much thinner than the traditional chili con carne made popular in Texas. Cincinnati chili includes some unexpected flavors—allspice, cloves, cinnamon, and cocoa—alongside more traditional chili spices, such as garlic, cumin, cayenne, and chili powder.

You will be hard-pressed to find a Cincinnati chili parlor that will provide you with a recipe, however. Apparently, the almost two hundred chili parlors in Cincinnati have an agreement with one another not to share their recipes, which is why you won't find one in this book; but no chili book is complete without at least a mention of Cincinnati chili and its cult-like status.

Luckily, many other restaurants across the U.S. and Canada were more than happy to share their secrets with me. Traditionalists will be pleased to find recipes for real Texas chili from the Cosmos Café in Houston and Clark's Outpost in Tioga, Texas. Many of the recipes in *Killer Chili* are refreshingly innovative, such as the bison chili from Meriwether's in St. Louis, the sun-dried tomato and chorizo chili from the Sherwood House Restaurant in Canmore, Alberta, and the catfish and red bean chili from the Crown Restaurant in Indianola, Mississippi. There are also several healthy, hearty vegetarian recipes for cooks who want to omit meat from their chili.

I hope these recipes inspire you to have fun and to experiment in your own kitchen, not just with chili but with anything you cook!

CHILI 101

Chile Peppers

The thing that makes chili chili is, of course, the chile pepper. Chile peppers are any of the hot varieties from the capsaicin-producing *Capsicum* genus, which is a member of the nightshade family. They are beloved all over the world and are a major component of not only Tex-Mex cooking, but also Thai, Indian, Chinese, Indonesian, Korean, South American, Caribbean, and other cuisines. Each kind of chile is different from the next, from the smoky chipotle to the deceptively deli-cate-sounding Scotch bonnet, one of the hottest chiles in the world. Their shapes and colors vary, too, and if you are lucky enough to have access to farmers' markets or specialty grocery stores, you know the sight of a rainbow of chile peppers is a real treat.

What chiles have in common with one another is their heat, and it's that same heat that elevates what might otherwise be just beef or vegetable stew into the chili stratosphere. The chemical compound capsaicin, natu-rally occuring in chiles, is quite fascinating. When you ingest a chile, the capsaicin sends a pain sensation to the brain, which releases feel-good endorphins, the body's natural painkillers. Not only that, capsaicin is hydrophobic, which means that drinking water is inef-fective in quelling the heat; reach for milk or a piece of buttered bread instead. Alcoholic beverages work, too, which is perhaps why beer is often the preferred accompaniment to chili.

While all chiles pack a punch, the degree of that punch and the flavor they imbue vary. The Scoville scale, created by chemist Wilbur Scoville in 1912, specifically measures the heat of chile peppers by determining the amount of capsaicin present in each pepper. Chiles are assigned a range of Scoville heat units (SHUs). For instance, Tabasco sauce, made from the Tabasco chile, has between 600 and 800 SHUs. The hottest chile in the world, the Dorset Naga, has between 800,000 and almost two million SHUs. Nearly every recipe for chili that you'll encounter will use chili powder in addition to or in place of the actual pep-pers. Typically, chili powder is made from dried ground chiles, usually the ancho variety, plus cayenne pepper, cumin, and other spices. When a recipe calls for peppers, it's good to know what you're dealing with before you start. Here's a (very) brief primer on some of the chiles and sweet peppers used in the recipes in this book:

Bell pepper (0 SHUs): Sweet, with no heat.
New Mexico red (500-2,500 SHUs): Also known as Ana-heim; very mild.
Poblano (1,000–1,500 SHUs): Very mild; one of the most pop-ular chiles grown in Mexico. Anchos are dried poblanos.
Pasilla (1,000–4,000 SHUs): Mild to medium-hot; chilacas are a fresh variety of pasillas, and chile negros are a dried variety.
Jalapeno (2,000–8,500 SHUs): One of the most popular chiles. Chipotles are smoked, dried jalapenos, often pack-ed in adobo sauce.
Cayenne (30,000–50,000 SHUs): Moderately hot; most often dried and ground.
Serrano (10,000–23,000 SHUs): A very "meaty" Mexican variety; moderately hot.
Habanero (100,000–350,000 SHUs): One of the world's hot-test chiles, with a fruity aroma and flavor; cultivated in Mexico's Yucatan peninsula, parts of Latin America, and the American Southwest.
Scotch bonnets (100,000–350,000 SHUs): One of the world's hottest chiles and a derivative of the habanero; found in the Caribbean.

Always wash your hands in hot, soapy water after han-dling chile peppers. Better yet, wear rubber gloves.

Chiles can cause immediate skin irritation for some people, and the oils from the peppers stay on your hands for longer than you realize, so be sure you've scrubbed away every last trace before getting your fingers near your eyes and other delicate body parts. The area at the base of the stem and the seeds are the most potent parts of chile peppers, and most recipes say to remove them. Unless you're a culinary daredevil, it's not a step you want to forget.

Beans

Many recipes call for dried beans, which must be soaked overnight. (Canned beans are often a fine substitute in a pinch.) If you forgot or don't have time to soak dried beans overnight, follow these instructions from Mary Ellen Hope, owner of Bishop's Chili in Chicago, to cook them more quickly:

> Boil 2 large pots of water. Place the dried beans in a separate large stockpot. Pour one pot of boiling water over the beans and stir. Let them soak until the water cools, then drain, leaving the beans in the stockpot. Add the second pot of boiling water to the beans, soak until water cools, and drain the beans.

Cooked beans are usually added to chili close to the end of the cooking process; if they cook too long, they can disintegrate into a mushy mess.

General Cookin' Tips

Famous chili aficionado H. Allen Smith believed that all "civilized" chili cooks make chili in an iron kettle, but that's just not practical in most kitchens. However, you should definitely use a large, heavy pot for most of the recipes in *Killer Chili*. While many of the recipes are scaled back

from their original restaurant-size forms, most still make a gallon of chili or more—perfect for a large group or for leftovers. Chili can be eaten as a side dish or an entrée, and serving sizes vary, but for our purposes, each serving is approximately one cup, a standard entrée size. With anything you cook, always use the best ingredients you can find and afford—it really makes a difference. It's a common misconception that soups, particularly those that utilize a lot of ingredients as chili does, are just a means of ridding the refrigerator of leftovers, and that the quality of the ingredients doesn't matter. With anything you cook or bake, the sum will only be as good as its parts.

Chili takes some time between the soaking, the chopping, and the simmering, but it's worth it. Don't cut the cooking time short if you want the best result. If the instructions say to let the chili simmer for three hours, let it simmer for three hours. Chili is the gift that keeps on giving, too; it will taste even better a day or a few days after you've made it, as the time allows all of the flavors to really meet and mingle. If you have leftover chili, it freezes and reheats beautifully.

Chili is a great way to experiment with ingredients you may not use often, or at all. Make a pact with yourself: If you can't quickly find a certain chile, spice, or cut of meat, search for it. Visit ethnic grocery stores you pass on your way home from work but never go to. Introduce yourself to your neighborhood butcher and request the cut you need rather than grabbing the first available pre-wrapped item in the case. Throw away spices that are too old (yes, they age, too) and replace them with new ones. Order a high-quality chili powder or another spice online or from a specialty foods shop. With a little bit of time and effort, you'll be well on your way to being a modern-day chili queen (or king)!

DRY DOCK RESTAURANT & TAVERN

PORTLAND, MAINE

A Portland staple since 1983, the Dry Dock Restaurant & Tavern actually has two docks that overlook the scenic working waterfront. Located at the eastern end of busy Commercial Street in the Old Port section of the city, the Dry Dock is a favorite with locals and tourists.

Like all coastal New England towns, Portland is known for its plentiful seafood. Menus abound with local catches, and the Dry Dock is no exception. Diners can feast on peel-and-eat shrimp, a Maine crabmeat roll, fried clams, fried haddock, lobster and crabmeat clubs, and the famous shrimp Bloody Mary. There's plenty for land-lubbers to enjoy, too, including filet mignon, superb burgers, and Reuben and corned-beef sandwiches. Chowders and chili are another delicious draw for diners hoping to ward off the coastal chill.

Developed by Dry Dock cook Shirley Tubbs, Shirley's Chili is a fairly traditional, hearty chili with ground beef, tomato, and beans. Dry Dock manager Jeannine LaRochelle explains that the secret behind it is that they allow individual or groups of ingredients to cook and simmer awhile before adding more ingredients. The process of layering flavors creates a well-spiced, dynamic chili that scintillates on the palate.

Shirley's Chili

1 pound ground chuck

1 tablespoon kosher salt

1 tablespoon freshly ground black pepper

1 green bell pepper, seeded and diced

$\frac{1}{2}$ red bell pepper, seeded and diced

2 jalapeno peppers, seeded and diced

1 large white onion, diced

4 large or 6 small cloves garlic, minced

2 bay leaves

1 tablespoon dried oregano, crumbled

1 teaspoon dried basil, crumbled

5 tablespoons chili powder

2 tablespoons ground cumin

$\frac{1}{2}$ teaspoon ground red pepper

One 28-ounce can tomatoes, diced

One 28-ounce can tomato sauce

One 28-ounce can red kidney beans, drained and rinsed

Diced onions, shredded cheddar cheese, tortilla chips (optional)

Heat a heavy $4\frac{1}{2}$-quart saucepan on medium-low heat until hot, then add the ground chuck and half of the salt and black pepper. (You should use salt and pepper throughout the cooking process when adding the ingredients.) Add the bell peppers, jalapenos, onion, and garlic to the beef and sauté until the beef is cooked through, 10 to 15 minutes. Add the bay leaves, spices, and remaining salt and pepper, stir well, and cook for 4 to 5 minutes. Add the tomatoes, tomato sauce, and kidney beans. Stir, then simmer for 2 hours. During the last 30 minutes of cooking, check the seasoning and add more salt and black pepper if needed.

Serve in a crock with diced onions, melted Cheddar cheese, and tortilla chips, if desired. *Serves 12.*

GENERAL COOKIN' TIP

★ Be sure to cook the spices for 4 to 5 minutes before adding the tomatoes, tomato sauce, and kidney beans, to cook off the rawness of the spices.

MAINE DINER

WELLS, MAINE

New England carries the unfortunate stigma of being, to put it delicately, a little less hospitable than other parts of the country. Whoever came up with that stereotype clearly never made it to the Maine Diner, where friendliness is next to godliness. Myles Henry and his two brothers opened the diner in 1983 with a simple plan to serve good, home-cooked food in a clean, friendly atmosphere. It seemed like a winner of an idea, but it took several years for it to catch on with customers. Once people tried the Maine Diner, though, it became an instant favorite, and since the early '90s, has maintained its reputation for being bustling—and serving good, home-cooked food in a clean, friendly atmosphere. It's not uncommon for Boston residents to make the seventy-mile drive north once a week or more, even on their lunch hours. Even the *Today* show crew made the trek.

Along with meat loaf, potpie, and a score of seafood dishes (it is Maine, after all), Maine Diner's chili is a popular constant on the menu. Like much of the food served at the diner, the recipe hails from Henry's mother, though it's been "tweaked" a bit. "For a non–Tex-Mex restaurant," Henry says, "we have great chili." His secret? "Chili is like pizza," he says. "There are so many way to make it. The key for us is to make it in small batches, and make it often."

Maine Diner Chili

1 pound ground chuck

1 small onion, coarsely chopped

1 clove garlic, minced

1 tomato, diced

1 48-ounce can chili con carne

1 48-ounce can kidney beans, drained

$1/3$ cup prepared horseradish

2 cups water

$1/2$ teaspoon salt

$1/2$ teaspoon freshly ground black pepper

1 tablespoon dried thyme, crushed

1 teaspoon chili powder

$1/2$ teaspoon red pepper flakes

1 dash Tabasco sauce

In a large, heavy pot, sauté the ground chuck over medium heat until cooked through, 10 to 15 minutes. Drain and return to the pot. Add the onion and garlic, then add all the remaining ingredients and stir. Cook over low heat for 3 hours, stirring occasionally. *Serves 8.*

GENERAL COOKIN' TIP

★ This chili is even better reheated the next day—and the day after that!

GOURMET CAFÉ

GLENS FALLS, NEW YORK

Every neighborhood should have a restaurant like the Gourmet Café in Glen Falls. Owner and chef Francis Willis and his wife, Tracy, have created a casual, cozy spot and a menu with fresh salads, soups, panini, and other fare, most of which Willis prepares on a long table in the dining room. Donning crisp chef's whites, Willis surrounds himself with bowls of vegetables, spices, meats, and other ingredients, and has several sauté pans going on a series of tabletop gas burners. Diners watch Willis toss, turn, and flip their food, and during warmer months, patrons can sample

Willis' creations at an outdoor sidewalk table.

Willis' main priority is giving his customers what they want, and true to form, his versatile Southwestern Black Bean Chili can easily become vegetarian if you delete the beef and broth and use more beans. Just add 1 cup dried kidney beans, 1 cup lentils, and 1 cup green split peas to the black and Great Northern beans. Soak the beans and the split peas (but not the lentils) in cold water for at least 8 hours, though overnight is preferred, then follow the rest of the original recipe for a delicious, meat-free meal.

Southwestern Black Bean Chili

1½ cups dried black beans

1 cup dried Great Northern beans

¼ cup olive oil

2 tablespoons minced garlic

1 large white onion, diced

1 green bell pepper, seeded
   and diced

1 red bell pepper, seeded and diced

2 pounds lean ground beef

¼ cup hot chili powder

¼ cup mild chili powder

2 teaspoons ground cumin

2 teaspoons ground coriander

1 teaspoon cayenne pepper

1 teaspoon red pepper flakes

1 teaspoon freshly ground black pepper

2 tablespoons sugar

1 tablespoon dried oregano, crumbled

1 tablespoon kosher salt

4 cups (16 ounces) dark beer,
   preferably stout or porter

2 cups beef broth

Two 28-ounce cans diced tomatoes

One 28-ounce can tomato purée

Shredded Cheddar cheese, diced red
   onion, and sour cream for garnish

Pick over and rinse the beans. Soak the beans in a large pot filled with cold water for at least 8 hours or preferably overnight; do not drain. Transfer the pot to the stove. Cook the beans slowly over medium heat until tender, about 1 hour. Drain the beans and set aside.

In a large, heavy pot, heat the olive oil over medium heat and sauté the garlic, onion, and peppers until slightly soft. Add the beef and sauté until fully cooked. Add the spices, sugar, oregano, and salt and stir until they start to stick to the bottom of the pan. Add the beer and stir, cooking until the volume of beer reduces by half. Add the beef broth and the diced and puréed tomatoes and stir thoroughly. Add the cooked beans, reduce the heat to low, and simmer for 2 hours. Serve in bowls, topped with the cheese, onion, and sour cream. *Serves 6 to 8.*

PORTSMOUTH BREWERY

PORTSMOUTH, NEW HAMPSHIRE

The iconic '80s sitcom *Cheers* taught us that bars are not just for drinking, but for community and friendship building, as well. Pushing that concept just a bit further are brewpubs, where visitors can meet, mingle, and actually get to watch—not just taste—beer brewing right before their eyes. Microbrews and the brewpubs that serve them are known for being inventive and often a bit irreverent, and the Portsmouth Brewery in New Hampshire is typical in that regard.

After working as head brewer at the Northampton Brewery in Massachusetts, owner Peter Egelston brought his brewing know-how to the Granite State.

Portsmouth and its sister company, Smuttynose Brewing Company, now produce a variety of brews, including Black Cat Stout, "Wild Thang" Wild Rice Ale, and Old Brown Dog Ale. Many of the restaurant's dishes are made with beer, including the brewery's chili, which uses Smuttynose's Old Brown Dog Ale. But non–New Hampshire residents shouldn't despair—a different brand or variety will make a fine substitute. When you think about it, beer and chili are about as perfect a match as peanut butter and jelly. Hot and spicy foods practically beg for a cold, frosty beer to be consumed on the side; the Portsmouth Brewery just cuts to the chase and adds some to the pot.

Portsmouth Brewery Chili

1 tablespoon canola oil

1 pound ground chorizo sausage

1 pound lean ground beef

2 cups diced onions

2 cups diced green bell peppers

$\frac{1}{4}$ cup minced garlic

One 48-ounce can chopped tomatoes

1 tablespoon ground cumin

1 tablespoon ground coriander

1 tablespoon chili powder

1 teaspoon cayenne pepper

1 teaspoon kosher salt

12 ounces Smuttynose Old Brown Dog Ale or another English brown ale

4 cups cooked kidney beans, drained

In a large, heavy pot, heat the oil over medium heat. Add the meat, and brown. Add the onion, pepper, and garlic and simmer until soft. Add the tomatoes, seasonings, and ale. Simmer for 1 to $1\frac{1}{2}$ hours, stirring occasionally to keep the chili from sticking to the pot. Add the kidney beans and stir before serving. *Serves 8 to 10.*

GENERAL COOKIN' TIP

★ If you want a spicier chili, double the amount of cayenne pepper.

★ For a thicker chili, add tomatoes slowly until chili reaches the desired consistency.

ROSEBUD DINER

SOMERVILLE, MASSACHUSETTS

Located in a restored historic diner car in Somerville, a Boston suburb, the Rosebud Diner was added to the National Register of Historic Places in 1999. This listing is appropriate; one of the reasons visitors love the Rosebud so much is that it's barely changed since its 1941 opening. After more than sixty years, the diner is still full of chrome, swiveling counterstools, and old-fashioned comfort food delivered quickly to the tables by sassy, sharp-tongued servers. Over the years the menu has changed a bit to keep up with the times; veggie burgers certainly weren't standard fare in the '40s! The diner also has a full bar to accommodate those looking to indulge in a Bloody Mary with their scrambled eggs and home fries.

Another relatively new feature is Tom Norton, who started cooking at the Rosebud in 1999. He developed his chili recipe about twenty years ago, however, and brought it with him to the diner. Like everything at the Rosebud Diner, Norton's recipe is neither fussy nor fancy, but don't let the simple recipe fool you— Norton's chili is a savory treat. The chef and part-time musician debuted his chili years ago at a local annual music festival, where hundreds of hungry fans and musicians gobbled the stuff up, and it's now a continual bestseller at the diner. He urges home cooks to practice his "trial-and-error" technique with the recipe, as well, particularly when it comes to the spices, the amounts of which are listed "to taste."

Rosebud Chili

2 $\frac{1}{2}$ pounds ground beef

3 $\frac{2}{3}$ cups canned red kidney beans, drained

3 $\frac{2}{3}$ cups canned baked beans, drained

2 stalks celery, chopped

$\frac{1}{2}$ large white onion, chopped

$\frac{1}{2}$ cup sliced jalapeno chiles

$\frac{1}{2}$ large red bell pepper, seeded and chopped

$\frac{1}{2}$ large green bell pepper, seeded and chopped

6 $\frac{1}{2}$ cups diced fresh tomatoes

Ground cumin to taste

Chili powder to taste

Seasoned salt to taste

Freshly ground black pepper to taste

Dash of Tabasco sauce, or to taste (optional)

In a large, heavy pot, combine the beef with just enough water to cover it. Bring to a simmer over medium heat and cook until browned. Drain. Add the beans, celery, onion, chiles, peppers, and tomatoes and cook until tender. Season with the cumin, chili powder, seasoned salt, and pepper. For added spice, add a dash (or more) of Tabasco. *Serves 10 to 12 people.*

VANILLA BEAN CAFÉ

POMFRET, CONNECTICUT

Chili and vanilla beans don't often find themselves mentioned in the same breath, but people are certainly talking about the chili at the Vanilla Bean Café. Locals in Pomfret, Connecticut, have known about the eatery's chili for years, but those outside this small town really started to take notice after the New York *Times* wrote about it. The café has also received accolades from other prestigious publications, including the Boston *Globe* and *Yankee* magazine, which called it "one of the outstanding reasons to visit New England."

Owner Barry Jessurun and his family opened the Vanilla Bean Café in 1989 in a restored, early-nineteenth-century barn. Back then, the café seated only sixteen people, but since then has expanded its capacity to fit ninety people inside and forty outside. Their philosophy for their restaurant, as laid out when they started the place, was to "create a place where we would feel comfortable and serve food that we would want to eat. If we wouldn't eat it, we certainly wouldn't serve it." Easily surpassing this standard, the menu is chock-full of inventive, delightful fare.

The Vanilla Bean cooks its chili slowly for several hours to allow the array of flavors to meld. This chili uses two kinds of meat—lean ground beef and spicy chorizo sausage—to make the soup a perfect hearty, satisfying choice for lunch or a light supper.

Award-Winning Chili

2 pounds lean ground beef

2 teaspoons plus 1 1/2 tablespoons chili powder

1/2 teaspoon plus 1/2 tablespoon ground cumin

2 teaspoons black pepper

1/2 teaspoon cayenne pepper, or to taste

2 drops Tabasco sauce

2 links fresh smoked Mexican chorizo sausage

1 tablespoon minced jalapeno chile

3 cloves garlic, minced

1 onion, chopped

4 stalks celery, chopped

1/2 red bell pepper, seeded and chopped

1/2 green bell pepper, seeded and chopped

One 16-ounce can tomato sauce

One 28-ounce can tomato purée

One 28-ounce can diced tomatoes

One 16-ounce can kidney beans, drained

In a large, heavy skillet, combine the ground beef with the 2 teaspoons chili powder, the 1/2 teaspoon cumin, the black pepper, cayenne pepper, and Tabasco sauce. Cook over medium heat until the meat is browned. Drain, reserving 3 tablespoons of the fat.

Slice the chorizo in half lengthwise and cut into bite-size pieces. In a large, heavy pot, cook the chorizo over medium-high heat for 4 to 5 minutes. Add the 1 1/2 tablespoons chili powder, the 1/2 tablespoon cumin, the jalapeno, garlic, onion, celery, bell peppers, and reserved fat. Cook until the vegetables are tender. Add the tomato products, reduce the heat to medium, and cook for 15 to 20 minutes, stirring occasionally. Stir in the cooked beef and kidney beans and simmer for 2 hours. Serve in crocks with tortilla chips, shredded Cheddar cheese, and scallions, if desired. *Serves 10 to 12.*

GENERAL COOKIN' TIP

★ Chili is known and loved for its versatility. It freezes very well, so any leftovers can be stored in the freezer for up to 6 months and reheated when desired.

MAREMMA

NEW YORK, NEW YORK

After one glance at the recipe for chef Cesare Ca-sella's chili, you know you're in for something new. The Tuscan chef delights in catching diners off-guard, piquing their interest, if not their suspicion, and then delivering inventive, unexpected dishes that pack a wallop. He's been doing it for years at his Manhattan restaurant, Maremma. The name comes from a cattle-breeding region on the Tuscan coast in Italy, and the whole eatery is an homage to cowboys. Pictures of Tuscan cowboys adorn the walls, and old-time country tunes wail throughout the dining room. When he's not in the kitchen, Casella often roams about his restaurant wearing—you guessed it—cowboy boots. And the req-uisite bull's horns are mounted on the wall.

Advocates of Texas bowls of red or Cincinnati five-ways might pooh-pooh this chili for its lack of traditional chili qualities, but whatever you may think, it all comes down to one thing: This chili is tasty. It has strong Italian influences, including fresh rosemary and sage, pancetta, and fennel seeds—be-loved flavors in Mediterranean cooking. But Casella blends those with garam masala (a spice most often found in Indian cuisine), coffee, chocolate, and more traditional chili ingredients, such as beef, tomatoes, and chili powder. This is cooking (and eating!) at its best, when the food becomes more than a meal and is elevated to an experience.

Cesare Casella's Tuscan Chili

1 red onion, quartered

1 small carrot, chopped

1 jalapeno chile, chopped

1 tablespoon chopped fresh rosemary

1/2 tablespoon chopped fresh sage

2 stalks celery, chopped

4 cloves garlic

2 ounces pancetta, chopped

8 strips bacon

3 tablespoons olive oil

2 pounds beef chuck or skirt steak,
   cut into 1-inch strips

Salt and freshly ground pepper to taste

1 tablespoon garam masala

One 16-ounce can tomato purée

1/2 teaspoon ground cumin

1/2 teaspoon fennel seed

1 1/2 tablespoon chili powder

1 small potato, peeled and cut into
   1/2-inch cubes

2 cups water

1 cup brewed dark-roast coffee

5 cups beef broth

2 cups canned red or kidney
   beans, drained

3/4 ounce unsweetened chocolate,
   chopped

Freshly grated Parmesan cheese
   for garnish

1 small white onion, coarsely chopped

1 avocado, peeled, pitted, and
   coarsely chopped

Preheat the oven to 400°F. In a food processor, chop the onion, carrot, jalapeno, rosemary, sage, celery, garlic, and pancetta. Place the bacon on a sided baking sheet and bake in the oven until crisp, about 15 minutes. Remove, dry with paper towels, and set aside. In a large, heavy saucepan, combine the olive oil and chopped-vegetable mixture and cook over medium-high heat for 10 minutes.

In a large bowl, season the meat with the salt, pepper, and garam masala. Add to the saucepan and cook for 12 minutes, stirring occasionally. Add the tomato purée, cumin, fennel seed, chili powder, potato, and water. Cover and simmer for 20 minutes. Add the coffee and 2 cups of the beef broth and cook for another 20 minutes, stirring constantly. Add the beans and 1 cup of the beef broth and simmer for 30 minutes. Add the remaining 2 cups broth and simmer for 15 minutes. Add the chocolate and cook for another 20 minutes, stirring occasionally. Crumble the bacon. Serve the chili garnished with the Parmesan, crumbled bacon, onion, and avocado. *Serves 6.*

MAIN STREET EURO-AMERICAN BISTRO & BAR

PRINCETON, NEW JERSEY

Main Street was first established as a high-end catering business in 1984 in the Kingston neighborhood, at the north end of Princeton. In 1992, owner Sue Simpkins expanded it to include the bistro and bar, and Princetonians think of Main Street as their "kitchen away from home." The clientele of Main Street is as eclectic as the menu, with Princeton students and professors, New York commuters, and local businesspeople making up a corps of regular patrons. "It's a place where neighbors gather," Simpkins says. "It's really comfortable; it's not glitzy, not city-chic, and not chain fastfood. You know you're going to run into friends, and you know you're going to have good food. A good loaf of bread, a good bottle of wine, how can you lose with that?"

Part of that good food is Main Street's chili, which started out on the catering menu twenty-five years ago and has now become a fixture on the bistro menu. "It's a well-established chili in this neighborhood," Simpkins says. "There are no miraculous secret ingredients, but it's a combination of parts." Like the bistro, the chili could perhaps be described as Euro-American, with its use of sweet Italian sausage and Burgundy wine. The American part? Simpkins' own herb concoction, a special blend of ground fiery chiles and mild peppers, herbs, and spices, which she brought with her when she moved to Princeton from Seattle, and aptly named Wild West Chili Spice.

Main Street Chili

Olive oil for browning
$1/2$ pound sweet Italian sausage
$2 1/2$ pounds ground beef
3 onions, chopped
1 clove garlic, minced
One 28-ounce can peeled plum tomatoes
One 6-ounce can tomato paste
$1/4$ cup Burgundy or other dry red wine
2 tablespoons fresh lemon juice
$1/3$ cup Wild West Chili Spice (see tip)
1 teaspoon salt
$1/4$ cup minced fresh parsley
$1/4$ cup minced fresh dill
$1 1/2$ cups beef broth
One 16-ounce can kidney beans, drained
Sour cream and shredded cheddar cheese (optional)

In a large, heavy pot, heat the oil over medium heat and brown the sausage and beef. Drain well. Crumble the beef, cut the sausage into $3/8$-inch pieces, and return to the pan. Add the onions and cook over medium heat until the onions are translucent. Add all the remaining ingredients. Cover and simmer over low heat for 30 minutes.

Serve with sour cream, shredded Cheddar cheese, and wedges of warm corn bread, if desired. *Serves 10.*

GENERAL COOKIN' TIP

★ Main Street Wild West Chili Spice can be purchased through Main Street's website (www.mainstreetprinceton.com), but you can use the following recipe to make a zesty substitute: $1/4$ cup chili powder, 3 tablespoons ground cumin, 1 tablespoon dried basil, 1 tablespoon dried oregano, $1 1/2$ teaspoons ground black pepper, and 2 teaspoons salt. Mix together. Store unused seasoning in a covered jar.

SALAMANDRA

CARLISLE, PENNSYLVANIA

Salamandra is one of those great neighborhood restaurants that are hard to leave. Between the cheery goldenrod-colored walls hung with paintings by local artists, the smell of freshly baked bread, and the warm glow emanating from the wood-fired brick oven in the back section of the tiny bistro, it's no wonder Salamandra's regulars have been coming for lunch or dinner once a week or more for years. Nothing here is too over-the-top or overdone; it's simple food made with super-fresh ingredients. Owner and chef Sally Powers, who creates each menu with co-chef Quentin Zell, is an advocate of minimalist cooking and believes that unfussy dishes using high-quality ingredients equal a better meal.

Salamandra's food firmly falls into the Italian category, but Zell has the freedom to experiment and dabble, and the customers love it when he does. One of Zell's most popular chilis features grilled chicken and poblano chilis. Poblanos are green, fairly mild, and heart-shaped, and they're usually stuffed with meat or cheese in the Mexican dish *chiles rellenos*. Here the peppers blend beautifully with the strong, fresh flavors of garlic, onion, cumin, chili powder, tomato, and fresh cilantro.

Poblano and Grilled Chicken Chili

3 tablespoons olive oil

1 large red onion, finely chopped

3 poblano chiles, seeded and finely chopped

3 garlic cloves, minced

One 16-ounce can chopped tomatoes, with juice

2 tablespoons dark chili powder

$1/2$ teaspoon ground cumin

1 tablespoon minced fresh cilantro

Salt and freshly ground pepper to taste

7 ounces canned kidney beans, rinsed and drained

7 ounces canned black beans, rinsed and drained

10 to 12 ounces skinless, boneless chicken, grilled and cut into small cubes

2 cups chicken broth

1 tablespoon tomato paste

5 green onions, finely chopped

1 cup shredded Gruyère cheese

In a large, heavy saucepan, heat the oil over medium heat. Add the onion and po-blanos. Cook for 3 to 4 minutes, stirring occasionally, until the onion just softens. Add the garlic and continue cooking until the onion begins to color. Add the tomatoes with their juice, chili powder, cumin, and cilantro. Bring just to a boil, reduce the heat, cover, and simmer for 10 minutes. Season with salt and pepper. Add the kid-ney beans, black beans, and grilled chicken. Stir in the chicken broth and tomato paste. Cover and continue simmering for 30 to 40 minutes, stirring occasionally, until the vegetables are tender. Taste and adjust the seasoning. Serve hot, topped with the green onions and shredded cheese. *Serves 6 to 7.*

GENERAL COOKIN' TIPS

★ Have all your ingredients assembled and prepared before you start cooking. It makes your time in the kitchen more enjoyable and less rushed.

★ If you have time, roast or smoke the poblanos to add a bit more kick.

SIDECAR BAR & GRILLE

PHILADELPHIA, PENNSYLVANIA

The Sidecar Bar & Grille in downtown Philadelphia is a quintessential neighborhood bar. Located on the corner of Twenty-second and Christian Streets, the building looks modest from the outside, but owners Adam and Jennifer Ritter have created a sleek, urban-chic watering hole inside. Local papers have touted the Sidecar as one of the city's best-kept secrets, for both its food and its cocktails. Adult libations are certainly the biggest draw here, including the Sidecar the bar is named for, fashionable martinis, and old-school Pabst Blue Ribbon.

Another crowd-pleaser is the chili, developed by chef Richard Freedman. "People dig it," he says. "And if you're the cook, it's nice because it doesn't take all day, you can freeze some for next time, and it still tastes like it came from the Rio Grande on a chuck wagon." Freedman stresses that his recipe, like all recipes, is a guideline, and that cooks should experiment with the ingredients at will. For instance, if you prefer a bit of smokiness, add a tablespoon of chipotle powder. Or add a few tablespoons of stone-ground cornmeal to the sautéed vegetables for a thicker, stick-to-your-ribs texture. You can substitute pinto or black beans for kidney beans, or venison or wild boar for the beef. For an extra kick, add a shot (or so) of tequila with the beer.

Sidecar Bar & Grille Chili

1 tablespoon corn, peanut, or canola oil

1 large green bell pepper, diced

1 large yellow onion, diced

3 tablespoons minced garlic

1 tablespoon ground cumin

1 tablespoon cayenne pepper

3 tablespoons chili powder

1 tablespoon ground ancho chile

3 tablespoons adobo seasoning

2 tablespoons salt

1 tablespoon freshly ground black pepper

3 pounds ground beef

2 cups lager

One 28-ounce can crushed tomatoes

One 28-ounce can kidney beans, rinsed and drained

Sour cream, shredded cheddar cheese, sliced green onion, and chopped fresh cilantro (optional)

In a large, heavy pot, heat the oil over medium-low heat and sauté the bell pepper, onion, garlic, and seasonings until tender. Form the ground beef into large, thin burgerlike patties and sear in batches in a smoking hot iron skillet until the meat is very dark brown. Flip over and sear the other sides. Then break up the meat a bit and brown the inside of the patties. Using a slotted spoon, transfer the cooked meat to the pot. Drain and discard as much fat as you can from the skillet before you add another batch of beef.

Once all the beef is seared and in the pot, add the lager, cover, and bring to a boil. Add the tomatoes and reduce the heat to a simmer. Add the kidney beans and simmer for about 20 minutes. Taste and adjust the seasoning. Serve in bowls with tortilla chips and top with shredded Cheddar cheese, sour cream, sliced green onion, and fresh cilantro, if desired. *Serves 11.*

GENERAL COOKIN' TIP

★ If you plan on freezing your chili, cool it to room temperature before transferring it to the freezer to prevent bacterial growth.

MIDWESTERN U.S. · KILLER CHILI

CAFÉ LATTE

ST. PAUL, MINNESOTA

Don't let the name fool you. Patrons at Café Latte can enjoy much, much more than just coffee. This Twin Cities eatery serves a huge variety of fresh food, beverages—including the lattes, of course—and desserts in an open, airy cafeteria-style setting. It also houses a gallery, with rotating exhibits of paintings, sculptures, pottery, wood carvings, and other artwork throughout the year.

Patrons can pick up gourmet boxed lunches with sandwiches of dilled egg salad, smoked turkey, tuna salad, or baked ham; fresh fruit or vegetable salads; and sweet chocolate hearts for dessert. Café Latte starts baking bread for their sandwiches—organic sourdough, whole-wheat, ten-grain, and rye—in the middle of the night to get ready for the morning rush. For dinner, people can dine on hand-crafted fresh-baked pizzas, complemented by an array of well-priced wines. There's even daily afternoon tea, complete with finger sandwiches, desserts, and a pot of tea—as close to Great Britain as you can get in Minnesota.

Café Latte also channels the American Southwest with its chicken salsa chili, which features chicken breasts and a variety of vegetables and spices, and is finished with the fresh zing of lime and cilantro. Hominy, which is made from dried corn kernels, thickens the chili and adds an earthy flavor.

Chicken Salsa Chili

3 tablespoons olive oil

1 pound boneless, skinless chicken breasts, cut into 1-inch pieces

1½ cups chopped yellow onions

½ teaspoon red pepper flakes

1 tablespoon minced garlic

2 teaspoons minced jalapeno chile

1½ cups chicken broth

3 tablespoons chili powder

One 28-ounce can whole tomatoes, broken up, with juice

One 28-ounce can tomato purée

Two 15-ounce cans dark red kidney beans, drained

One 15-ounce can hominy, drained

⅓ cup chopped fresh cilantro

2 tablespoons fresh lime juice

Chopped red onion, sour cream, shredded cheddar cheese, tortilla chips (optional)

In a large, heavy pot, heat the olive oil over medium heat and sauté the chicken until opaque throughout. Add the onions, reduce the heat to medium-low, and cook for 3 minutes, or until the onions are tender. Add the pepper flakes, garlic, jalapeno, chicken broth, chili powder, tomatoes, tomato purée, beans, and hominy. Simmer for 15 to 20 minutes, until everything is incorporated and the chili thickens to the desired consistency.

To serve, add the cilantro and lime juice, and adjust the seasoning to taste. Ladle the chili into bowls; if desired, top with sour cream, chopped red onions, shredded Cheddar cheese, and tortilla chips. *Serves 2 to 3.*

FAMOUS DAVE'S

MINNEAPOLIS, MINNESOTA

Dave Anderson first fell in love with ribs as a kid in Chicago. His father brought the succulent meat home in his lunch pail, and it was love at first bite for the young boy. In the twenty-five years that followed, Anderson searched high and low for the country's best barbecue, tasting smoked meat at thousands of rib joints in the barbecue capitals of Memphis, Kansas City, Texas, the Carolinas, and his native Chicago. His destiny was clear: He needed to open a place of his own.

The first Famous Dave's opened in 1994 in the small lakeside town of Hayward, outside Minneapolis. Visitors from the Twin Cities began traveling to Famous Dave's BBQ Shack in droves, and eventually convinced him to open a restaurant in Minneapolis. More than a decade later, Famous Dave's is now an institution, not just as a barbecue joint but also as a hoppin' blues club.

Famous Dave's has done an exceptional job translating its barbecue greatness to its other forte, chili. They won't reveal the recipes for their Steak & Burger Seasoning or BBQ sauce, but you can buy the concoctions directly from their website, www.famousbbq.com. Vibrant and exciting, their chili has a staggering blend of flavors and textures. Treat your family and friends to it, and you'll become famous for chili, too.

Famous Dave's Route 66 Truck Stop Chili

3 pounds lean coarse-ground beef

2 teaspoons Famous Dave's Steak & Burger Seasoning (see page 32)

5 tablespoons chili powder

1 teaspoon coarse-ground black pepper

4 teaspoons ground cumin

2 teaspoons Maggi seasoning

1 tablespoon dried basil

1 teaspoon garlic powder

1 cup chopped celery

1 cup chopped onion

1 cup chopped green bell pepper

1 large jalapeno chile, seeded and minced

Two 16-ounce cans hot chili beans with broth

One 22-ounce can tomato juice

One 15-ounce can diced tomatoes with juice

One 15-ounce can tomato purée

One 10-ounce can beef broth

3 tablespoons Famous Dave's BBQ Sauce (see page 32)

2 tablespoons Kahlúa liqueur

2 tablespoons Worcestershire sauce

Shredded cheddar cheese, chopped onion (optional)

In a large, heavy pot, combine the ground beef, Steak & Burger Seasoning, chili powder, black pepper, cumin, Maggi seasoning, basil, and garlic powder and mix well. Cook over medium heat until the ground beef begins to turn a crusty brown, stirring frequently. Add the celery, onion, green pepper, and jalapeno. Cook until the vegetables are tender, stirring frequently. Add the chili beans, tomato juice, tomatoes, tomato purée, broth, BBQ sauce, Kahlúa, and Worcestershire sauce and mix well. Simmer to your desired consistency, stirring occasionally. Ladle into bowls and serve with shredded Cheddar cheese, chopped onion, corn bread and/or crackers, if desired. *Serves 6 to 8.*

BAR ABILENE

MINNEAPOLIS, MINNESOTA

You might expect a place called Bar Abilene to be located in Texas, not Minnesota, and that's the idea. The restaurant describes itself as a "Texas margarita grill," and its logo features a letter A that looks straight from the hot end of a branding iron.

Though it may not feel like Texas outside in the dead of a harsh Minnesota winter, Bar Abilene conjures up a true Lone Star experience. Guacamole is made tableside by the servers, and the bartenders whip up a mean margarita—twenty-five different varieties, in fact. The cuisine is dubbed "cowboy fusion," and includes cayenne-dusted calamari with arugula, wasabi, and smoked-tomato aioli, combining Asian, Southwestern, and Mediterranean flavors on one plate.

The menu changes seasonally, but an assortment of inventive quesadillas, tacos, seafood, and burgers are always available.

What Tex-Mex restaurant would be complete without chili? Bar Abilene's rendition is not exactly Texas-style—there are beans and tomatoes involved—but it features ground beef, poblano and chipotle chiles, beer, and a ton of spices. Some of the other ingredients, such as tamarind pulp, ancho purée, and masa harina, are perhaps not items you typically keep in your pantry, but a visit to a Latino specialty store or through the ethnic-food aisles of your grocery store should do the trick. You can also order them from a variety of online purveyors.

Bar Abilene Chili

3 tablespoons canola oil

2 pounds ground beef

1$\frac{1}{4}$ tablespoons minced garlic

1$\frac{1}{4}$ tablespoons chili powder

1$\frac{3}{4}$ tablespoons ground cumin

$\frac{1}{4}$ teaspoon ground coriander

1 teaspoon cayenne pepper

$\frac{1}{4}$ teaspoon dry mustard

1$\frac{3}{4}$ tablespoons paprika

3$\frac{3}{4}$ teaspoons salt

$\frac{1}{8}$ teaspoon freshly ground black pepper

$\frac{1}{2}$ cup ancho purée

2$\frac{1}{2}$ cups Guinness beer

2$\frac{1}{4}$ cups chicken broth

1$\frac{3}{4}$ cups salsa roja (red salsa)

5$\frac{1}{2}$ tablespoons tamarind pulp

2 cups cooked black beans, drained

1 tablespoon molasses

3 to 4 chipotle chiles, minced

1 poblano chile, finely chopped

4 cups canned chopped tomatoes

$\frac{2}{3}$ cup masa harina

In a large, heavy pot, heat 2 tablespoons of the oil over medium heat and brown the beef. Add the garlic and all the herbs and spices, stirring to combine. Make a small "well" in the meat, add the remaining 1 tablespoon oil, and fry the ancho purée for about 2 minutes. Stir in the beer and cook to reduce for 10 minutes. Add the broth and salsa roja and simmer for 20 minutes. Add the tamarind pulp, beans, and molasses and simmer for 2 hours.

Stir in the chiles, tomatoes, and masa harina and bring to a boil. Stir to blend, then serve. *Serves 4 to 6.*

AMY'S CAFÉ

—— MADISON, WISCONSIN ——

Chili is heralded for its filling, stick-to-your-ribs heartiness, and vegetarian chili can be—and often is—just as gratifying as its meaty counterparts. Plus, as a meal, you can't get more versatile: Chili can contain almost anything you want to eat.

The vegetarian chili at Amy's Café in Madison, Wisconsin, is both versatile and hearty. Amy's is not a vegetarian restaurant, but its menu boasts pleasing meatless options, including a Mediterranean platter of house-made hummus and tabbouleh. In the meatless-

but-not-exactly-healthy category is the Wisconsin take on fried mozzarella: fried cheese curds.

What separates vegetarian chili from vegetable stew? The spices, of course. Amy's chili features the standard chili flavors—cumin, chili powder, and cayenne pepper—combined with chili beans, roasted red peppers, onions, and your choice of fresh vegetables. Be sure to add vegetables with the longest cooking times to the pan first and those with the shortest cooking times last.

Amy's Café Vegetarian Chili

$1/4$ cup olive oil

2 small onions, chopped

1 tablespoon minced garlic

2 tablespoons chopped fresh parsley

1 teaspoon dried oregano

1 teaspoon dried basil

$1/2$ cup roasted red bell pepper

1 tablespoon ground cumin

1 tablespoon chili powder

Pinch of cayenne pepper

4 cups chili sauce

3 cups cooked chili beans

1 cup cooked kidney beans

3 cups mixed chopped vegetables (such as green beans, broccoli, mushrooms, bell peppers, and corn kernels)

In a large, heavy pot, heat the oil over medium heat. Add the onions, garlic, parsley, oregano, basil, and red pepper and sauté until tender, 5 to 10 minutes. Add the cumin, chili powder, cayenne pepper, chili sauce, and beans and heat through.

While the bean mixture cooks, put the vegetables in a medium saucepan. Add enough water to cover the vegetables and simmer over medium heat until almost tender, 10 to 15 minutes. Drain and add to the bean mixture. Bring to a boil, then reduce the heat to medium-low and simmer for 15 minutes. *Serves 6 to 8.*

MIDWESTERN U.S.
★ ★
KILLER CHILI

BISHOP'S FAMOUS CHILI

WESTMONT, ILLINOIS

The Windy City may have the Sears Tower, but the Chicago suburb Westmont has Bishop's Chili. In 1925, Mary Bishop was cooking chili at legendary Ole's Chili, but got fired after making changes to the recipe. Out of work, Bishop opened her own chili joint on Chicago's west side. Her son, George, joined his mother's venture, and his business savvy helped the meager chili parlor expand into other parts of Illinois, including Forest Park and Westmont. Eventually George's daughters married, and their husbands wanted to continue the Bishop chili legacy.

Currently, only the Westmont location remains open, but the business is still a family operation; Mary Bishop's great-granddaughter, Mary Ellen Hope, now runs the business. And they're still making the same recipe that Grandma Bishop created more than eighty years ago, and serving it in a few different ways: in chili mac (chili over spaghetti), on hot dogs, in tamales, and by itself in a bowl.

That said, the folks at Bishop's Chili were a little hesitant to give up their family secret. Hope, though, decided to craft a recipe that is very much like the original Bishop's Chili—you'll have to travel to Westmont, Illinois, for the real thing. Whether you've tasted the original Bishop's Chili or not, this delicous version will not disappoint.

"I Can't Believe It's Not Bishop's Chili" Chili

1 pound boneless choice beef bottom roast, cut into $1/2$-inch dice
$1/2$ pound lean boneless pork trimmings or boneless end-cut pork roast,
    cut into $1/2$-inch dice
2 tablespoons salt
1 or 2 ancho chiles
6 japone chiles (small dried red peppers)
1 pound white onions, cut into small chunks
2 tablespoons garlic powder
2 tablespoons chili powder
5 pounds dried pinto beans, soaked overnight, rinsed, and drained

In a large stockpot, combine the beef, pork, and salt and add water to cover. Bring to a boil. Skim off any foam, cover, and reduce the heat to a simmer. Cook for 2 hours. Meanwhile, soak the ancho and japone chiles in warm water to cover.

In a food processor, process the onions to a coarse purée. Empty into a bowl and add the garlic powder and chili powder. Drain the ancho and japone chiles, purée them in the food processor, and add to the onion mixture.

Drain the meat. Purée the pork in the food processor and add to the onion mixture. Return to the stockpot and stir. Add the rinsed beans, cover, and simmer for 2 hours, or until the beans are soft, stirring often to prevent burning. Water may be added if needed. Purée the cooked beef in the food processor and add to the chili.

Let the chili cool to room temperature, then cover and refrigerate overnight. Reheat over low heat to serve. *Serves 8.*

BIG BOPPER'S

MARBLEHEAD, OHIO

When a restaurant's logo features a flaming chile pepper, you know you're in for a serious bowl of chili. And at Big Bopper's, they do it up right. Owner Ken Kostal developed his Island Heat Chili recipe over twenty years ago, after seeing an advertisement for a chili cook-off in Cleveland, where he competed and took the grand prize. Turns out he had a secret weapon: a family recipe of his manager at the time. "It was either his mom's or grandmother's," Kostal says.

Since then, Kostal has become somewhat of a chili guru, enjoying fame and acclaim in chili circles all over the country; he's racked up more awards and honors for his chili than he can count. He used to split his time between Big Bopper's and trekking to chili contests in every corner of the United States, but now he sticks closer to home. Still, he runs nine charity cook-offs in Ohio and is a judge at the world championship. "I took the avenue of being the chili chairman," he says.

With chili as amazing as his, he can call himself whatever he wants. Kostal describes his Island Heat as "not too spicy, with good flavor." And he gladly shares his chili philosophy: Real chili does not have beans in it—serve them on the side if you must; chili should be cooked slowly; and it's good with and on anything, including nacho chips, potato skins, burgers, and omelets. Chili is also perfect just by itself.

Island Heat Chili

5 pounds ground beef

8 cups water

2 cups tomato paste

4 cups chopped onions

$1\frac{1}{2}$ teaspoons minced garlic

$2\frac{1}{2}$ teaspoons Worcestershire sauce

$8\frac{1}{2}$ tablespoons chili powder

5 teaspoons ground cumin

1 tablespoon salt

5 teaspoons freshly ground black pepper

1 teaspoon red pepper flakes

$1\frac{1}{4}$ teaspoons ground allspice

Sour cream, minced jalapenos, and shredded cheddar cheese (optional)

In a large, heavy skillet, brown the meat in batches over medium heat. Drain off all the fat. Transfer the meat to a large, heavy pot. Stir in the water, tomato paste, onions, garlic, $7\frac{1}{2}$ tablespoons of the chili powder, and all the other remaining ingredients. Bring to a simmer and cook for $2\frac{1}{2}$ hours. Stir in the remaining 1 tablespoon chili powder and cook 30 minutes to 1 hour longer, or until the desired consistency is reached. Serve with beans, sour cream, minced jalapenos, and shredded Cheddar cheese, if desired. *Serves 15.*

GENERAL COOKIN' TIP

★ The chili will start out thin, but will thicken as it cooks.

MARKET STREET GRILL

WABASH, INDIANA

Indiana is mostly known for basketball, race cars, and John Mellencamp, but the Hoosier State also produces some mighty fine chili. Some of the best in the state can be found in the small town of Wabash, at the Market Street Grill.

Owner Bill Gerding—or "Wild Bill," as he's known on the chili circuit—professes a deep love and reverence for chili. He's been making it for more than twenty-five years and has competed in—and won—cook-offs all over the country. Now a chili emeritus of sorts, he serves as an organizer and judge. A member of the International Chili Society, Gerding has some pretty strong opinions about the do's and don'ts of good chili. Beans? Yes. Tomatoes? Yes. Macaroni? No.

His award-winning Indiana Red utilizes both beans and tomatoes, as well as ground chuck and round steak—typical for Midwestern chili—as well as beer, onions, peppers, kidney beans, and lots of spices, including garlic powder, cumin, and paprika. As a nod to the cowboys and ranch hands of yore, Gerding and his staff serve the chili in miniature black iron kettles. While the Indiana red isn't knock-your-socks-off spicy, it does have a kick, and Gerding aptly urges on his menu, "If you're looking for wimpy, order corn flakes."

Wild Bill's World-Famous Indiana Red "Chili with an Attitude"

1/4 cup canola oil

2 1/2 pounds coarse-ground chuck

1 1/4 pounds round steak, cut into 1/2-inch dice

1/4 cup hot chili powder

1 1/2 tablespoons ground cumin

1/2 tablespoon paprika

3/4 teaspoon garlic powder

3/4 teaspoon black pepper

1 1/2 tablespoons salt

1/2 tablespoon sugar

3/4 cup beer

3/4 cup water

3 cups tomato sauce

6 cups diced tomatoes

6 cups cooked dark red kidney beans with broth

1 1/4 cups diced onions

3/8 cup diced green bell pepper

In a large, heavy pot, heat the oil over medium heat and brown the meat. Mix the spices, salt, sugar, beer, and water together, then add to the pot with the meat and oil. Reduce the heat to low and cook for 5 minutes. Add the tomato sauce, tomatoes, beans and broth, onions, and bell pepper. Simmer for 4 hours, stirring occasionally to prevent sticking.

Place the chili pot into an ice bath to cool. Cover and refrigerate overnight.

Before serving, remove the film of oil floating on top of the chili and discard. Reheat the chili and serve. *Serves 12.*

THE PAINTED GIRAFFE CAFÉ

ST. LOUIS, MISSOURI

Granted, most people don't go to zoos to eat, and why should they? Zoo food typically means hot dogs and soft pretzels served from a cart, a necessity to maintaining one's energy when flitting from the lemurs to the cheetahs to the reptiles. The Painted Giraffe Café at the St. Louis Zoo, however, has raised the bar. Chef—yes, an actual chef!—Jerry Chollet creates quick bites that are adult, kid, and palate friendly. Hot dogs are available, but so are Thai turkey wraps, meatball sandwiches, BLTs on croissants, fish and chips, and a great chili.

Painted Giraffe's food helped propel the St. Louis Zoo to the No. 1 spot in *Zagat* and a listing in *Parenting* magazine's survey of the best zoos in the United States. The café opened in 1988, and Chollet took over the reins at the upscale cafeteria a few years later. The chili—house made, like the rest of their soups and desserts—is not too spicy but full of zesty, savory flavor, and home cooks will appreciate its simple ingredients and preparation. It's the perfect chili to serve to a large number of hungry guests.

Painted Giraffe Café Chili

5 pounds ground beef

1 1/4 cups diced onion

2/3 cup diced green bell pepper

Two and a half 28-ounce cans diced tomatoes, with juice

Two 40-ounce cans kidney beans, with juice

8 cups rich beef broth

2 teaspoons garlic powder

1 1/2 teaspoons red pepper flakes

2 teaspoons freshly ground black pepper

3 tablespoons ground cumin

1/2 bay leaf

2 teaspoons dried oregano

2 1/2 tablespoons chili powder

2 1/2 teaspoons salt

In a large, heavy pot, brown the meat in batches over medium heat. Drain and discard all but 1/4 cup of the fat. Transfer the meat to a bowl. In the same pot, sauté the onion and pepper in the reserved beef fat until tender. Add the tomatoes and kidney beans and stir well. Add the broth and spices, reduce the heat to low, and cook for 2 to 3 minutes. Add the cooked meat. Bring to a boil, then reduce the heat to low and simmer for 30 to 45 minutes, skimming the fat from the surface as needed. *Serves 14.*

GENERAL COOKIN' TIP

★ This chili is not too thick, so oyster crackers complement it well to make a great meal.

MERIWETHER'S

ST. LOUIS, MISSOURI

The food at Meriwether's, a fine-dining restaurant in the Missouri History Museum, is so delicious that even the Food Network has taken notice. Named for Meriwether Lewis, of the Lewis and Clark expedition, which passed through Missouri on its famous journey, the restaurant was dubbed one of the country's Best Museum Restaurants by the Network's show *Best Of*. After a day of discovery in the museum, which houses the original Louisiana Purchase document, a replica of Charles Lindbergh's famous airplane *The Spirit of St. Louis*, and personal items once belonging to William Clark, Chuck Berry, Tina Turner, Miles Davis, Charles Lindbergh, and Scott Joplin, history buffs can rest and refuel in Meriwether's.

Instead of the usual ground beef, Meriwether's chili recipe calls for ground bison meat. The restaurant uses Missouri-raised buffalo, but bison farms are cropping up in nearly every corner of the United States and Canada. It's worth the effort to find and support local farms, if possible. Buffalo was once a free-roaming species that survived solely on prairie grasses, so look for meat that comes from free-range or grass-fed bison versus grain fed for a product that's more natural and healthier. Bison is tender and lean—great in burgers and fantastic in chili. The combination of the meat, two kinds of beans, and a mélange of spices and vegetables will become a favorite in no time, making your home the new place where the buffalo roam.

Bison Chili

2 to 3 tablespoons canola oil

$1/2$ cup diced onion

$1/2$ poblano chile, roasted, seeded, and diced (optional)

1 stalk celery, diced

$1/2$ cup diced red bell pepper

2 tablespoons minced garlic

$1\,1/4$ pounds ground bison meat

4 tablespoons dark chili powder

$1/2$ tablespoon ground cumin

1 teaspoon cayenne pepper

52 ounces canned diced tomatoes

52 ounces canned kidney beans

52 ounces canned black beans

$3/4$ cup tomato juice

In a large, heavy pot, heat the canola oil over medium heat and sauté the onion, chile, celery, bell pepper, and garlic until the onion is translucent. Add the meat and cook until brown. In a small bowl, mix together the chili powder, cumin, and cayenne and add to the meat and vegetables. Add the tomatoes, beans, and tomato juice. Simmer for 40 minutes, stirring occasionally, and serve. *Serves 10.*

MIDWESTERN U.S. ★ KILLER CHILI ★

ESKIMO JOE'S

STILLWATER, OKLAHOMA

Eskimo Joe's is the quintessential college-town hangout; even *The Sporting News* and *Sports Illustrated* deemed it one of the top college sports bars in the country. Conveniently located just one block from Oklahoma State University's campus, its wall are hung with huge televisions to facilitate game-day crowds, and of course, they serve a lot of beer.

One thing that sets Eskimo Joe's apart from other college sports bars, however, is that the food is very good. No pathetic pizza or stale nachos here—the fare is a bit more sophisticated than that. Dishes include a pecan smoked-pork shoulder sandwich, a variety of chicken sandwiches called "fowl things," and chili, which is piled onto hot dogs, nachos, burgers, and that Midwest and Southern favorite, Fritos pie—a mound of Fritos corn chips smothered with onions, tomato, and cheese in addition to the chili.

Eskimo Joe's recipe is a perfect game-day chili. It's tasty, with a bit of bite from the green chiles, and couldn't be easier to make. It can easily be doubled for bigger crowds, and you can serve it by itself or as a topping for other foods.

Eskimo Joe's World-Famous Chili

3 pounds ground beef

Two 4-ounce cans peeled whole green chiles

One 10-ounce can diced tomatoes with green chiles

One 10-ounce can spicy chili beans

Two 8-ounce cans tomato sauce

$3/4$ cup chopped green bell pepper

$3/4$ cup chopped onion

$1/4$ cup chili powder

1 tablespoon seasoned salt

1 tablespoon ground cumin

2 teaspoons dried oregano, crumbled

1 tablespoon freshly ground black pepper

$1/2$ teaspoon red pepper flakes

1 teaspoon salt

$1^{1}/4$ cups water

In a large, heavy skillet, brown the meat over medium heat. Add all the remaining ingredients and simmer until the vegetables are tender, about 1 hour, until the chili reaches 165°F. *Serves 4.*

GENERAL COOKIN' TIP

★ After browning the meat, you can put all the ingredients in a slow cooker on low for about 8 hours, instead of simmering the mixture on the stove.

SOUTHERN U.S.
KILLER CHILI

VIA CUCINA

WASHINGTON, DISTRICT OF COLUMBIA

Residents of the metropolitan Washington, D.C., area are lucky enough to have six Via Cucina market-cafés to choose from, though the Pennsylvania Avenue location was the first. Each café offers incredibly fresh and flavorful Mediterranean-style breakfast and lunch options. They emphasize the merging of the European-style marketplace and café, where people can have their pick of ripe produce and freshly baked breads, then find those same ingredients at the corner bistro in a salad, soup, sandwich, or pastry.

One inventive item on the Via Cucina menu is White Turkey Chili. It uses two kinds of turkey—turkey breast slices and ground turkey—for a real punch of flavor and texture. Combined with the turkey are the bite of jalapeno chiles and Tabasco, the smooth nuttiness of pearl barley, two types of beans, and subtle flavors of dried marjoram and summer savory, a sweet, mild herb perfect for meat dishes. This chili is a lighter alternative to standard red chilis, but it's just as satisfying.

White Turkey Chili

2 tablespoons canola oil

$\frac{1}{2}$ cup finely chopped onion

1$\frac{1}{2}$ tablespoons minced garlic

4 teaspoons ground cumin

1 pound turkey breast slices, cut into $\frac{1}{2}$-inch dice

$\frac{1}{2}$ pound ground turkey

3 cups chicken broth

$\frac{1}{4}$ cup pearl barley

2 tablespoons minced jalapeno chile

1 teaspoon dried marjoram

1 teaspoon dried summer savory

One 15-ounce can cannellini or Great Northern beans, drained and rinsed

One 15-ounce can chickpeas (garbanzo beans), drained and rinsed

Several dashes Tabasco sauce

Salt and pepper to taste

Chopped green onions, shredded Cheddar cheese, and sour cream for garnish

In a large, heavy saucepan, heat the oil over medium heat. Add the onion and garlic and sauté until tender, about 5 minutes. Add the cumin and stir until fragrant, about 30 seconds. Add the diced and ground turkey and sauté until no longer pink, about 4 minutes. Add the broth, barley, jalapeno, marjoram, and summer savory. Cover and simmer, stirring occasionally, until the barley is almost tender, about 40 minutes. Add the cannellini and chickpeas. Simmer, uncovered, until the barley is tender and the chili is thick, about 15 minutes. Season with the Tabasco sauce, salt, and pepper. Serve with the green onions, cheese, and sour cream. *Serves 4.*

SOUTHERN U.S.
KILLER CHILI

THE ROOST

LEXINGTON PARK, MARYLAND

Contrary to what its name implies, poultry does not rule the Roost—ham does. Diners love the "old ham" sandwich, which may sound a bit unappetizing to the uninitiated, but is actually succulent. The St. Mary's County ham sandwich, crammed with kale and other veggies, is another specialty. And owner Bill Harris and his fellow Roost-ers are no slouches when it comes to cooking up some mighty fine chili, too.

Located in Lexington Park, Maryland, about sixty miles south of Washington, D.C., the Roost has enjoyed a loyal following for decades. Harris describes

Roost devotees as "a cult, but a good cult." He should know; before he bought the place, he'd been coming to the Roost since his teenage years. The décor is old-fashioned and quaint, qualities that infuse the menu. Most of the recipes are simple and venerable; some are as many as fifty years old. The chili recipe has been around for more than twenty-five years, Harris says. Though he calls the recipe "pretty basic," people adore the results. It's the perfect example of East Coast–style chili: a little bit sweet, a little bit hot, but chunky, satisfying, and full of flavor.

The Roost Chili

2$\frac{1}{2}$ pounds ground beef

$\frac{1}{2}$ large onion, diced

$\frac{1}{2}$ tablespoon dried oregano, crumbled

6 cups crushed tomatoes

6 tablespoons chili powder

2 tablespoons garlic powder

1$\frac{1}{2}$ cups ketchup

$\frac{1}{2}$ teaspoon red pepper flakes

6 cups cooked dark red kidney beans

In a large, heavy pot, sauté the beef, onion, and oregano until brown. Add all the remaining ingredients and simmer for about 1 hour, or until the chili is of the desired consistency. *Serves 15.*

GENERAL COOKIN' TIP

★ Bill Harris recommends using Schreiber- or McCormick-brand spices.

BISTRO 301

LOUISVILLE, KENTUCKY

Formerly known as Deke's Marketplace Grill, Bistro 301 provides inventive lunch and dinner offerings to the Louisville masses. It's been a downtown staple for years, and rightfully so. The menu is, as expected, composed of bistro-style dishes, and favorites include tortellini diablo, with chicken and Cajun sausage in a red pepper–cream sauce, and an Asian chopped salad. Plus, Bistro 301 offers Kentucky's favorite, a "hot Brown sandwich," made of roasted turkey and laden with bacon, a rich Mornay sauce, and grated Parmesan.

Diners dig Bistro 301's vegetarian Southwest Vegetable Chili. It's a cornucopia of fresh veggies: three kinds of bell peppers, onion, tomato, squash, and eggplant. The addition of black beans and some hot spices makes this chili so satisfying and so flavorful, you won't miss the meat. Besides being healthy and delicious, the best part of Bistro 301's chili is that it's quick and easy to prepare. The brunt of the work comes from dicing the vegetables, but the rest is a snap and takes under an hour.

Southwest Vegetable Chili

2 to 3 tablespoons canola oil
1 cup diced red bell pepper
1 cup diced yellow bell pepper
1 cup diced green bell pepper
1 cup diced yellow onion
1 cup diced yellow squash
1 cup diced eggplant
1 cup diced tomato
3 cups tomato sauce
1 cup cooked black beans
$\frac{1}{4}$ cup minced jalapeno chile
$\frac{1}{4}$ cup chipotle chile purée
3 tablespoons chili powder
1 tablespoon ground cumin
Salt and freshly ground pepper to taste

In a large, heavy skillet, heat the oil and sauté the peppers, onion, squash, eggplant, and tomato until the onion is translucent. Add all the remaining ingredients and simmer for 30 to 45 minutes. *Serves 4.*

WILLY B'S GOURMET SMOKEHOUSE

FRANKLIN, TENNESSEE

Bill Bayersdorfer, owner of Willy B's, knows food. As an infant, the Kentucky native ate so much and so often, his mother took him to a doctor to find out what was wrong with him. As a teenager, he put away six meals a day without ever getting fat. He helped his mother make pancakes on Saturday mornings, and especially loved cooking over campfires during Boy Scout camping trips.

Little did he know then that cooking over an open flame would eventually become his career. In the summer of 1993, Bayersdorfer began selling barbecue from an old New York City–style street cart in downtown Louisville, Kentucky. Just six weeks later, his ribs were voted the best in the Kentuckiana region. Since then, the business has relocated from the street cart to a stationary location in Tennessee, and the accolades continue to pour in. Bayersdorfer and his barbecue have been featured on the Food Network, in the New York *Times*, and on the *Today* show.

While the barbecue at Willy B's gets most of the acclaim, the chili is certainly not to be missed. (Neither is the decadent World-Famous Brownie.) Bayersdorfer's tips for the perfect chili? Use the finest, freshest ingredients you can find. He also suggests using lean meats and dark red kidney beans, which have a more robust flavor than the lighter ones. Lastly, be patient. "If the recipe says to simmer for two hours or four hours, do that," Bayersdorfer says. And, "Like any soup, it's best if it sits for a day, to give the ingredients an opportunity to marry."

Willy B's Red Chili

1 1/2 pounds lean ground chuck
1 pound lean spicy bulk sausage
1 pound onions, chopped
1 1/2 tablespoons minced garlic
3 cups tomato juice
12 cups chopped tomatoes with juice
1/4 cup chili powder, mixed with 6 cups water
2 1/2 tablespoons ground cumin
2 tablespoons salt
3/4 teaspoon cayenne pepper
12 cups cooked dark red kidney beans

In a large, heavy pot, brown the chuck and sausage over medium heat. When the meat is halfway cooked, add the onions and garlic and continue to sauté until the onions are translucent. Add the tomato juice, tomatoes, chili powder liquid, cumin, salt, and cayenne pepper and thoroughly stir to blend and incorporate all the flavors and seasonings. Simmer for 1 hour. Add the beans and simmer for 30 minutes. Serve. *Serves 15 to 20.*

GENERAL COOKIN' TIP

★ To make the chili spicier, marginally increase the amount of cayenne pepper.

SWEET AND SAVORY BAKE SHOP & CAFÉ
—WILMINGTON, NORTH CAROLINA—

As soon as the weather turns warm, East Coasters hear the call of the seashore, and many of the most popular summertime sand-and-sea meccas are located in the Carolinas. Besides its proximity to the ocean, Wilmington, North Carolina, is a tourist haven due to its immortalization in classic films—both versions of *Cape Fear*, and *Blue Velvet*—and teenybopper TV shows like *Dawson's Creek* and *One Tree Hill*. The town has the distinction of being nestled between the Cape Fear River and the mighty Atlantic. There's water, water everywhere, so it's fitting that

Dave Herring, owner of the Sweet and Savory Bake Shop & Café, calls his chili Saltwater Chili.

There's actually no saltwater in the chili, but it's full of seafood, namely shrimp, crabmeat, and clams. Herring tasted and cooked a multitude of different chili styles during the course of his "culinary travels" in New Mexico, Colorado, Georgia, New York, and much of the rest of the United States. Of his Saltwater Chili, he says, "All I've done is substitute the meat with seafood. The final product is just like regular chili. It's got the roasted chiles, the chili powder, everything else."

Saltwater Chili

2 tablespoons olive oil

1 large onion, chopped

1 tablespoon garlic, chopped

2 tablespoons canned green chile peppers, chopped

1 tablespoons jalepeno pepper, seeded and chopped

1 teaspoon red pepper flakes

$1/4$ teaspoon salt

$1/4$ teaspoon pepper

1 tablespoon Italian seasoning

1 tablespoon ground cumin

1 green bell pepper, seeded and chopped

1 red bell pepper, seeded and chopped

1 cup canned steamed clams, chopped

$1/2$ pound fresh shrimp, peeled and deveined, then chopped

1 cup canned or steamed claw crabmeat

$1^1/2$ cups diced tomatoes with juice

$1^1/2$ cups canned red kidney beans with broth

$1^1/2$ cups cooked Great Northern beans with broth

3 tablespoons chili powder

In a large, heavy pot, heat the olive oil over medium heat. Add the onion and garlic and sauté until the onion is translucent. Add all the remaining ingredients, except the tomatoes, beans, and chili powder. Stir well. Add the tomatoes, beans, and chili powder. Cook for about 30 minutes, until the shrimp is pink and everything else is thoroughly heated. Taste and adjust the seasoning. Serve. *Serves 6.*

GENERAL COOKIN' TIP

★ Wait until close to the end of the cooking process to add the chili powder so the ingredients don't stick to the bottom of the pot and give the chili a burnt taste.

SOUTHERN U.S.
KILLER CHILI

ATLANTA FISH MARKET

ATLANTA, GEORGIA

The Atlanta Fish Market is not really a market, but a restaurant. The moniker is a bit of a misnomer, but the freshness that the word "market" implies is no misrepresentation. Voted Best Seafood Restaurant by *Atlanta* magazine, the place, which resembles an old train station, feels welcoming and comfortable, and the menu is outstanding. It's printed twice a day to make sure customers have their pick of the freshest fish. Executive chef Robert Holley was trained in French provincial cuisine, but his talents work beautifully in a Southern seafood spot. His selections include a variety of sushi, and feature such unusual fish as Indian River redfish, Arctic char, and Caribbean triggerfish.

Holley's Cape Cod Seafood Chili is one of his more inventive recipes. It includes several standard chili ingredients—jalapenos, chili powder, kidney beans, and tomatoes—but instead of using beef or pork, Holley utilizes scallops, shrimp, and cod. The concoction teases the palate with a combination of flavors and textures. The result is an utterly satisfying and unforgettable chili.

Cape Cod Seafood Chili

3 tablespoons olive oil

1 onion, diced

2 jalapeno chiles, seeded and diced

2 red bell peppers, seeded and diced

1 green bell pepper, seeded and diced

1 yellow bell pepper, seeded and diced

6 garlic cloves, minced

2 tablespoons salt

2 tablespoons chili powder

1 teaspoon freshly ground black pepper

1 teaspoon red pepper flakes

3 bay leaves

1 teaspoon ground allspice

6 tablespoons tomato paste

1 cup (8 ounces) bottled clam juice

$3^1/_2$ cups crushed tomatoes

One 15-ounce can kidney beans

4 ounces dark chocolate, chopped

$^1/_2$ cup chopped fresh cilantro

$^1/_2$ cup chopped fresh parsley

$1^1/_2$ pounds bay scallops

$1^1/_2$ pounds bay (cocktail) shrimp

One 6- to 8-ounce cod fillet, cut into chunks

In a large, heavy pot, heat the olive oil over medium heat. Add the onion, chiles, peppers, and garlic and sauté for 2 to 3 minutes. Add the salt, chili powder, black pepper, red pepper, bay leaves, and allspice and stir well. Add the tomato paste and stir for 2 minutes. Add the clam juice and crushed tomatoes and bring to a simmer. Add the beans, chocolate, cilantro, and parsley.

Taste for seasoning and add more if necessary. Add the scallops, shrimp, and cod and cook for 3 to 5 minutes, or just until the scallops and cod are opaque through-out. *Serves 6 to 8.*

SOUTHERN U.S. KILLER CHILI

THE CROWN RESTAURANT

INDIANOLA, MISSISSIPPI

B. King may be this tiny Mississippi Delta town's most famous resident, but thanks to Evelyn Roughton—or Miss Evelyn, as her employees call her—catfish is Indianola's most famous food. In 1976, Roughton and her husband, Tony, opened an antiques shop with a small tearoom, which served just lunch and afternoon tea. In the late '90s, however, the Roughtons relocated and expanded their business to incorporate the Crown Restaurant and the connecting Taste of Gourmet gift shop, now located on the town's main street.

Catfish is king at the Crown—and all over the Delta, where the farm-raised catfish industry first began. In 1997, Roughton and her husband penned the cookbook *The Classic Catfish*, and there's little else on the menu besides the whiskered fish, but the preparations of it are mind-bogglingly varied: pâté, casserole, poached au gratin, rolls, Florentine, and pies. Roughton's smoked catfish pâté has won international acclaim, and she and the Crown have been featured on CNN and the Food Network, and in *Southern Living* and the Washington *Post*. A favorite recipe of Roughton's is her Red Bean and Catfish chili, of which she says, "Mmmm, you wouldn't believe how good it smells when you're cooking it."

Red Bean & Catfish Chili

2 tablespoons canola oil

1 large onion, minced

3 garlic cloves, minced

2 tablespoons chili powder

1 teaspoon ground cumin

$1/2$ teaspoon ground coriander

1 teaspoon ground cinnamon

1 teaspoon dried oregano, crumbled

$1/2$ teaspoon cayenne pepper

One 16-ounce can diced tomatoes with juice

1 large green bell pepper, seeded and diced

One 16-ounce can kidney beans, drained and rinsed

$1/2$ teaspoon salt

Freshly ground pepper to taste

1 pound catfish fillets, diced

In a large, heavy saucepan, heat the oil over medium heat and sauté the onion, garlic, chili powder, cumin, coriander, cinnamon, oregano, and cayenne pepper for 2 to 3 minutes, stirring constantly. Add the tomatoes and juice, green pepper, kidney beans, salt, and pepper. Stir for 1 minute. Add the diced catfish fillets and gently stir into the chili. Reduce the heat to low and simmer for 15 minutes. Serve immediately. *Serves 2 to 3.*

CLARK'S OUTPOST BARBECUE RESTAURANT

TIOGA, TEXAS

Texas is one of two key chili epicenters in the United States (Cincinnati is the other). Fans of Lone Star State chili, which traditionally includes beef and chile peppers but not tomatoes or beans, claim that their particular style is the only real chili. As they say, don't mess with Texas—particularly when it comes to the very heated and long-running debate over which style of chili reigns supreme.

Located fifty miles north of Dallas, Clark's Outpost Barbecue Restaurant in Tioga, as the name implies, is best known for its slow-cooked barbecue, but the chili here is the real deal, at least by Texas standards. Tioga is proud of taking things slow, and eight hours are needed to smoke the restaurant's ribs and three days to smoke its brisket.

Clark's Outpost chili involves a good deal of time, too, but the recipe is about as pared down as it gets—just beef, onions, chiles, herbs, and some water. It gets its flavor from long simmering and from chipotle chile peppers, which are warm and smoky, not lightning-bolt hot. Canned chipotles are packed in Mexican adobo sauce, a deep-red, piquant concoction of ground chiles, vinegar, and herbs. This chili requires time, but it's well worth the wait.

Beef Chili with Chipotles & Cilantro

2 pounds lean ground beef

2$\frac{1}{4}$ cups chopped onions

3 tablespoons ground cumin

3 tablespoons chili powder

1$\frac{1}{2}$ tablespoons garlic powder

1 tablespoon minced canned chipotle chile in adobo sauce (see tip)

2$\frac{1}{2}$ cups water, plus more as needed

1 cup minced fresh cilantro

Salt and freshly ground pepper to taste

Shredded Cheddar cheese and sour cream for garnish

In a large, heavy Dutch oven, sauté the beef and 2 cups of the chopped onions over high heat, stirring often and breaking up the meat with back of a spoon, until the beef is cooked through, about 10 minutes. Add the cumin, chili powder, garlic powder, and chipotle and sauté for 3 minutes. Mix in the 2$\frac{1}{2}$ cups of water and $\frac{1}{2}$ cup of the cilantro. Reduce the heat to medium-low. Partially cover and cook for 1$\frac{1}{2}$ hours, adding more water by $\frac{1}{4}$ cupfuls if the chili becomes dry. Season with salt and pepper. Mix the remaining $\frac{1}{2}$ cup cilantro into the chili. Ladle into bowls and garnish with Cheddar cheese, sour cream, and the remaining $\frac{1}{4}$ cup chopped onion. *Serves 6.*

GENERAL COOKIN' TIP

★ If you can't find canned chipotle chiles in your market, you can purchase them at Latin American groceries, specialty foods stores, and online.

COSMOS CAFÉ

HOUSTON, TEXAS

What makes chili chili? Answers vary from region to region and even person to person, but traditionally, combining chile peppers, some form of meat, and spices and cooking it all in a pot qualifies. The Cosmos Café may call their blend green chile soup, but this is about as chili as chili can be.

Texas is known for its chili and its music, and revelers can enjoy both at the Cosmos Café. The joint regularly hosts an eclectic lineup of live rockabilly, Western swing, R&B, and more, while the menu boasts Reuben sandwiches, house-made potato chips, and, of course, its award-winning green chile chili. Most of the soup's flavor comes from pork butt and poblano chiles—almost four pounds of pork and 1 1/2 pound of chiles, to be precise. Depending on which part of North America you inhabit, these green chile peppers, sometimes mistakenly called pasillas, can be purchased in supermarkets or Latino markets. In this recipe, poblanos are roasted for additional smokiness and depth of flavor, rounding out the delicious, traditional chili.

Green Chile Soup

1 1/2 pounds poblano chiles (about 6 large chiles)

3 3/4 pounds boneless pork butt (pork shoulder), trimmed and cut into 1-inch pieces

Salt and freshly ground pepper to taste

3 tablespoons all-purpose flour

3 tablespoons canola oil

3 cups coarsely chopped onions

6 large garlic cloves, minced

1 tablespoon dried oregano, crumbled

1 tablespoon ground cumin

5 cups chicken broth

One 14-ounce can diced tomatoes with juice

Char the chiles over a gas flame or under a broiler until blackened on all sides. Enclose in paper bag and let stand for 10 minutes. Peel and seed the chiles and cut into 1-inch pieces. Put the pork in a large bowl. Sprinkle with salt and pepper. Add the flour and toss to coat the pork.

In a large, wide pot, heat 2 tablespoons of the oil over high heat. Working in batches and adding more oil as needed, cook the pork until brown on all sides, about 6 minutes per batch. Use a slotted spoon to transfer the pork to a large bowl. Reduce the heat to medium. Add the onions to the pot and stir until tender, about 6 minutes. Add the garlic, oregano, and cumin and stir for 2 minutes. Return the cooked pork and any accumulated juices to the pot. Add the broth, chiles, and tomatoes with juice and bring to a boil. Reduce the heat and simmer, uncovered, stirring occasionally, until the chili thickens and the meat is very tender, about 2 hours. Taste and adjust the seasoning. *Serves 6.*

GENERAL COOKIN' TIP

★ For an authentic Tex-Mex experience, serve the chili with warm corn tortillas and bowls of chopped fresh cilantro, chopped green onions, and sour cream for garnish.

HOWLEY'S RESTAURANT

WEST PALM BEACH, FLORIDA

Since its inception in 1950, Howley's Restaurant has been one of West Palm Beach's most beloved dining spots. Patrons have been happily feasting on their sandwiches, cocktails, and all-day breakfast, including a massive egg sandwich that boasts two fried eggs, bacon or sausage, cheese, ham, and French fries packed into a kaiser roll. In 2005, the diner underwent a renovation that maintained its quirky, kitschy retro style while adding some more modern improvements, like a dancing hula-girl lamp and a new sign out front that declares Howley's motto: "Cooked in sight, must be right."

Chili is one of many things that Howley's does right. It's meaty and spicy, with two different kinds of chile peppers. A word of caution: Habanero and Scotch bonnet peppers are two of the hottest peppers in the world; jalapenos are mild in comparison. These spicy chiles can be found in most supermarkets, but plan accordingly if you prefer your food a bit less *caliente*. The seeds in chile peppers pack a wallop, so one way to lower heat is to scrape them out and discard them before dicing. Howley's chef Greg Schiff suggests passing around bowls of sour cream, guacamole, salsa, and chopped onions as garnishing possibilities.

Howley's Chili

2 red bell peppers, seeded and diced

2 green bell peppers, seeded and diced

2 white onions, diced, plus diced onion for garnish

$\frac{1}{3}$ cup canola oil

1 habanero or Scotch bonnet chile, seeded and diced

1 jalapeno chile, seeded and diced

3 pounds ground beef

Salt to taste

Freshly ground black pepper to taste, plus 1 tablespoon

1 tablespoon ground cumin

2 tablespoons Worcestershire sauce

5 cups crushed tomatoes

2 tablespoons cayenne pepper

3 tablespoons chili powder

2 tablespoons garlic powder

4 cups cooked red kidney beans

6 to 8 dashes Tabasco sauce

Sour cream, guacamole, and salsa for garnish

In a large, heavy pot, cook the bell peppers and 2 onions, covered, over medium-low heat, stirring occasionally, until tender. Add the oil and stir. Reduce the heat, add the chiles, and stir until the onions are translucent and the chiles are soft. Stir in the ground beef, salt, pepper to taste, cumin, and Worcestershire sauce. Cook until the meat is browned. Add the tomatoes and simmer for 30 minutes. Add the cayenne, the 1 tablespoon black pepper, the chili powder, and garlic powder. Add the kidney beans and Tabasco. Stir and add more seasonings, if desired. Cover and cook for at least 45 minutes. Let the chili stand for 20 minutes before serving. Serve in bowls and garnish with the sour cream, diced onion, guacamole, and salsa. *Serves 12.*

WESTERN U.S. ★ KILLER CHILI

WORLD CLASS CHILI

SEATTLE, WASHINGTON

World Class Chili is everything a great chili restaurant should be: It's fun, occasionally a little raucous, unpretentious, a tad boastful, and devoted to chili as if it were manna from heaven. One look at the mural depicting God giving man a bowl of chili, and you know you've come to the right place— and that's before you've sampled the chili.

Chili is part of owner Joe Canavan's family lore. He credits his grand-uncle Bill with bestowing on him his knowledge of chili cooking, and for motivating him to open his place in Seattle's Pike Place Market. Each day, Canavan and his crew serve at least four different varieties of chili, including a traditional Texas beef chili; a California-style chicken chili; a Cincinnati chili spiced with cinnamon, cloves, and chocolate; and a vegetarian lentil chili. The chili comes in "Texas-sized" or "Alaska-sized" bowls, and can be ordered in larger quantities for sizeable gatherings. Patrons can choose to have it with corn bread, tortilla chips, or crackers, and over pinto beans, black beans, brown rice, or seashell pasta.

In World Class Chili's vegetarian chili, the meat is replaced with lentils. Canavan does make a concession for meat-lovers, however, and suggests serving the chili over hot links or chorizo sausage, particularly the kind made at neighboring Uli's Famous Sausage. Vegetarians, fear not: Other than the serve-with-sausage option at the end, this recipe is completely free of any meat products.

World Class Vegetarian Chili

1½ tablespoons corn or peanut oil

1 small white onion, finely chopped

1 stalk celery, finely chopped

1 carrot, finely chopped

4 cloves garlic, minced

4 tablespoons chili powder

1 teaspoon cayenne powder

1 teaspoon black pepper, or more to taste

1 jalapeno chile, slits cut in skin

3 pounds lentils

1 teaspoon sugar

2 teaspoons ground cumin

1 tablespoon salt

1 teaspoon fresh lime juice

8 hot links, chorizo, or other spicy sausage, cooked and sliced (optional)

In a large, heavy pot, heat the oil over medium-high to high heat and cook the onion, celery, carrot, and garlic for 3 to 4 minutes. Add 2 tablespoons of the chili powder, ½ teaspoon of the cayenne, the black pepper, and jalapeno. Immediately add the lentils, stir, and then add cold water to cover the lentils by 1 inch. Bring to a boil, cover, and reduce the heat to a high simmer. In 25 minutes, check the lentils—they should be almost tender—and add a bit more water if necessary. Bring back to boil, then add the sugar, remaining 2 teaspoons chili powder, and the cumin. Cook at a high simmer for 10 minutes, then add the salt and the remaining 1½ teaspoons cayenne. Squeeze in the lime juice and cook for another 5 minutes. Let the chili sit for 10 minutes, and then serve over the sausage, if desired. *Serves 8.*

GENERAL COOKIN' TIPS

★ For a more interesting presentation, cut 8 acorn squash in half, scoop out the seeds, and slice a piece off the bottom of each piece so it sits flat in a roasting pan. Add ½ inch of water to the pan and bake the squash in a preheated 400°F oven for 1 hour, or until tender. Ladle the chili into the squash and enjoy!

★ For an extra-interesting flavor, substitute 2 tablespoons ground ancho chile for the chili powder.

COUGAR RANCH BED & BREAKFAST LODGE

MISSOULA, MONTANA

One reason people love chili so much is because it's one of the most versatile dishes ever invented. There are so many can-dos when it comes to chili, and so few don't-even-think-its; a perfect example is the chili from the Cougar Ranch Bed & Breakfast Lodge in Missoula, Montana, where guests can enjoy luxurious accommodations in a rustic, gloriously gorgeous setting. The ranch, like most everything in Big Sky Country, is sprawling, covering a 160-acre expanse of wilderness.

Instead of the usual beef, pork, or even chicken, Cougar Ranch's chili is made with elk, for an unexpected and unusual treat. Elk is lower in fat than even poultry and fish, and packed with protein. And it also happens to be delicious and less "gamey" than other wild game. Elk is a fairly standard provision in the western United States and in parts of Canada, but a real rarity most everywhere else. Never fear—the wonders of the Internet make it a snap to order elk meat shipped right to your door. Once you have the ground elk meat in hand (it browns just like ground beef), the rest of Cougar Ranch's recipe is fairly straightforward and hearty, with a touch of cocoa richness.

Hearty Elk Chili & Beans

1 pound dried red or pinto beans

2 pounds ground elk

2 garlic cloves, minced

1 large onion, chopped

1 green bell pepper, seeded and chopped

2 tablespoons all-purpose flour

One 28-ounce can tomatoes with juice

One 16-ounce can tomato sauce

1 cup water, plus more as needed

$\frac{1}{4}$ teaspoon salt

$\frac{1}{4}$ teaspoon freshly ground pepper

2 tablespoons ground cumin

1 tablespoon unsweetened baking cocoa

2 to 4 tablespoons chili powder

In a large, heavy pot, combine the beans with 4 cups of water and bring to a boil. Turn off the heat, cover the pot, and soak the beans for 3 hours. Drain, cover the beans with water, and bring to a boil. Turn the heat down and simmer the beans while preparing the rest of the ingredients.

In a large, heavy skillet, sauté the elk just until the meat is almost completely cooked. Add the garlic, onion, and green pepper and sauté until the onion is translucent. Add the flour and stir until the mixture forms a paste. Add the tomatoes with their juice, the tomato sauce, and the 1 cup water and stir until well mixed. Add the salt, pepper, cumin, cocoa, and chili powder. Bring to a boil and simmer for 15 minutes. Add to the simmering beans and continue simmering until the beans are tender, about $1\frac{1}{2}$ hours. Add water as needed during cooking to ensure that there is enough liquid to cover the beans and meat. Stir often, and serve when the chili reaches the desired taste and consistency. *Serves 5 to 6.*

WESTERN U.S. ★ ★ KILLER CHILI

UPTOWN CAFÉ

BUTTE, MONTANA

Since owners Barb Kornet and Guy Graham opened Uptown Café in 1985, the residents of the historic mining town of Butte have delighted in the restaurant's innovative big-city offerings. The décor is elegant yet comfortable, complete with walls adorned with work from regional artists and romantic lighting. Just as the Uptown's motto says, it's "civilized dining in the wild, wild West."

The Uptown Café has attracted scores of fans since its inception, including the *New York Times Magazine*, *Gourmet*, *Outside*, and renowned travel-and-food writers Jane and Michael Stern. The menu options include artichoke ravioli, beef Wellington, cioppino, and a blackened halibut steak for dinner, and a variety of sandwiches, pastas, soups, and other comfort foods for lunch. The Uptown serves its fantastic beef-and-pork chili for lunch every Monday, with a hunk of corn bread smothered in butter and honey; shredded Cheddar or Monterey jack cheese, diced onions, and sour cream also make delicious accompaniments, if you so desire.

Uptown Café Chili

¾ pound ground beef
¾ pound ground pork
1 cup finely diced yellow onions
1 red bell pepper, seeded and finely diced
1 green bell pepper, seeded and finely diced
1 teaspoon minced garlic
4 teaspoons good-quality chili powder
1 teaspoon cumin seeds
1 teaspoon ground cumin
1 teaspoon coarse-ground black pepper
1 bay leaf
⅛ teaspoon cayenne pepper
1 beef bouillon cube
One 28-ounce can diced tomatoes in purée
Two 12-ounce cans good tomato juice, such as Campbell's
One 24- to 28-ounce can red kidney beans, drained and rinsed

In a heavy 6-quart pot, combine the ground beef, ground pork, onions, peppers, garlic, chili powder, cumin seeds, ground cumin, black pepper, bay leaf, and cayenne pepper. Cook over medium heat until the ground meats are thoroughly cooked and the onions are soft, stirring often to break up the meat. Add the bouillon cube, tomatoes in purée, and tomato juice. Bring to a boil, then reduce the heat and simmer for 1 hour, stirring often. Add the kidney beans and cook until the beans are heated through. Remove the bay leaf, skim any fat from the top of the chili, and serve. *Serves 8 to 10.*

BAKERY BAR

PORTLAND, OREGON

Cakes may be king at Portland's Bakery Bar—even the eatery's motto proclaims, "Eat cake!"—but the place is not just for sweet treats. Here you can have your lunch—and eat cake, too. According to co-owner Jocelyn Barda, the Bakery Bar has become a gathering spot for "a lively mix of Portland residents," including local artists and designers, businesspeople, rowers exiting the Willamette River, and parents and kids who need a treat after a day adventuring at the nearby Oregon Museum of Science and Industry.

Sugar cravings can be conquered with cupcakes, cream puffs, pear-ginger caramel pie, and one of several decadent "cakes for two." Patrons looking for a non-dessert lunch can choose from fresh salads, soups, and sandwiches, including one overflowing with roasted vegetables and a delicate egg salad made with Dijon mustard, green onions, celery, and fresh basil. The Bakery Bar also serves homemade soups, and Portland residents love the chili. Made with lean ground turkey, it's a bit lighter than its beef counterparts, but it's definitely not a wimpy chili. Packed with spices (including cinnamon and thyme), tomatoes, garlic, beans, and a touch of brown sugar for sweetness, this chili might just make you forget to save room for dessert.

Bakery Bar Turkey Chili

2 tablespoons olive oil

1¼ cups chopped onion

5 cloves garlic, minced

1½ pounds ground dark-meat turkey

¾ teaspoon salt

1 tablespoon dried thyme, crumbled

2 tablespoons ground cumin

¼ cup chili powder

1 tablespoon ground cinnamon

1 tablespoon brown sugar

1 teaspoon cayenne pepper

Two 28-ounce cans whole tomatoes with juice, puréed in a food processor

1 bay leaf

Two 15-ounce cans pinto beans, drained

One 12-ounce can tomato paste

1 cup water

Shredded sharp cheddar cheese, chopped red or green onion,
     sour cream (optional)

In a heavy 8-quart pot, heat the olive oil over medium-low heat. Add the onion and garlic and cook until soft and beginning to brown. Add the ground turkey and cook until browned, stirring the meat frequently to break it up. Add the salt, thyme, cumin, chili powder, cinnamon, brown sugar, and cayenne, stirring well to combine, and cook for 3 minutes.

Add the tomatoes and juice, bay leaf, pinto beans, tomato paste, and water, stirring well to combine. Bring to a boil, then reduce the heat and simmer on low heat for 60 to 90 minutes, stirring occasionally. Remove the bay leaf. Serve with shredded sharp Cheddar cheese, chopped red or green onions, and sour cream, if desired. *Serves 10.*

GENERAL COOKIN' TIP

★ Adding the spices to the meat mixture before the liquids are added helps to bring out their full flavor.

THE DUNDEE BISTRO

DUNDEE, OREGON

Located in the middle of Oregon wine country in the northern Willamette Valley, the Dundee Bistro is a wine- and food-lover's paradise. The restaurant was founded in 1999 by one of Oregon's premier wine-making clans, the Ponzi family. The Dundee Bistro is actually one-third of the town of Dundee's Culinary Center, which also includes the Ponzi Wine Bar and Your Northwest, a specialty store selling regional foods and crafts.

The Ponzis modeled the Dundee Bistro after small, intimate eateries they've visited in wine regions all over the world, places where patrons can unwind and enjoy perfectly paired food and wine. Chef Jason Stoller Smith has created an exciting menu, which includes dishes, such as local Kumamoto oysters, roasted butternut squash soup with chanterelles, and Oregon petrale sole with spinach risotto, made with many organic and locally grown ingredients.

Chef Smith also gives traditional chili a creative Pacific Northwest touch. This creamy, savory chili features cannellini beans, fresh herbs, and the delicate, slightly sweet meat of Dungeness crab. These shellfish are readily available on the West Coast; other kinds of lump crabmeat may be substituted.

White Bean Chili with Dungeness Crab

2 pounds dried cannellini beans

$^1/_3$ cup olive oil

3 yellow onions, diced

1 small can peeled green chiles, drained and diced

1 tablespoon minced garlic

3 tablespoons ground cumin

$^1/_3$ cup chopped fresh cilantro

2 tablespoons chopped fresh oregano

$^1/_2$ teaspoon cayenne pepper

1 teaspoon ground cloves

1 whole ham hock

3 quarts chicken broth

1$^1/_2$ cups shredded Monterey jack cheese

3 cups sour cream

2 pounds fresh Dungeness crabmeat, picked over for shells

$^1/_4$ cup sliced bacon, cooked crisp, and croutons for garnish

Pick over and rinse the cannellini beans. In a large pot, cover the beans with 3 inches of water and soak overnight. Drain.

In a large, heavy pot, heat the oil over medium-high heat. Sauté the onions, chiles, and garlic until the onions are translucent. Add the cumin, cilantro, oregano, cayenne, and cloves. Add the drained beans, ham hock, and chicken broth and cook until the beans are tender, 2 to 3 hours. Add the cheese, stirring until well mixed. Add the sour cream, stirring until well mixed. Add the crabmeat, and stir well. Crumble the bacon. Top each serving with bacon and croutons. *Serves 12.*

NORTH COAST BREWING COMPANY

FORT BRAGG, CALIFORNIA

The North Coast Brewing Company in Fort Bragg, California, founded in 1988, holds the distinction of being one of the very first brewpubs in America. Located on the Mendocino coast, North Coast started out small and local. It now brews a variety of ales that reach thirty-six states—a lucky break for non-Californians. The beers, including Old Rasputin, Brother Thelonius, Blue Star, and PranQster Ale, are packed with flavor—a far cry from the watered-down brews coming from the bigger guys.

At some brewpubs, the food is an afterthought, but North Coast doesn't believe you have to sacrifice the quality of one for the other. Visitors who need something a bit more substantial than just beer in their bellies can order food at their Tap Room & Grill. What could go better with a pint than fresh Pacific oysters, Brazilian-style deep-sea scallops, wild-mushroom ravioli, porterhouse steaks, and beer's best friend, chili? The brewery's Route 66 Chili—named for the famous highway spanning the western United States—is so beloved that it was featured in *Bon Appetit* magazine. It's a combination of two chili types: Texas red and New Mexico green, and features pork butt, two kinds of chiles, and, not surprisingly, a bottle of amber ale.

Route 66 Chili

3 pounds boneless pork butt (pork shoulder), trimmed and cut into 1-inch pieces

All-purpose flour for dredging

$1/2$ cup olive oil

$3/4$ cup chopped onion

4 poblano chiles, seeded and chopped

$1/4$ cup minced garlic

One 28-ounce can diced tomatoes with juice

Two 19-ounce cans enchilada sauce

One 12-ounce bottle amber ale

One 7-ounce can diced green chiles

1 tablespoon ground cumin

1 tablespoon chili powder

Sour cream and sliced green onions for garnish

Dredge the pork in the flour to coat, shaking off the excess. In a large, heavy pot, heat $1/4$ cup of the olive oil over medium-high heat. Working in batches, brown the pork on all sides, about 8 minutes for each batch. Use a slotted spoon to carefully transfer the cooked pork to a large bowl. Add the remaining $1/4$ cup olive oil to the pot. Add the onion and sauté until translucent, about 4 minutes. Add the poblano chiles and garlic and sauté for 2 minutes. Mix in the pork, tomatoes with juice, enchilada sauce, ale, green chiles, cumin, and chili powder. Simmer over low heat, stirring occasionally, for about 1 hour, until the meat is tender and the chili thickens slightly. Serve with sour cream and sliced green onions. *Serves 8.*

WESTERN U.S. · KILLER CHILI

GLOBAL CHILI COMPANY

BOULDER, COLORADO

When owner Kyle Thomas, a former banker, lived in Singapore in the 1990s, he and his family invited friends to spend Thanksgiving with them. The day after Thanksgiving, instead of simply reheating leftover turkey, vegetables, and cranberries, Thomas put them all together, added Thai and Malaysian chile peppers, and made chili. Thomas' turkey chili was so divine that two visiting Colorado friends suggested he open chili kiosks at ski resorts in the States. Nearly a decade later, Thomas and his family moved back to the United States and took their friends' advice, opening Global Chili Company in downtown Boulder in 2005.

Rather than focusing on one type of chili, the menu at Global Chili Company, as its name implies, paints a broader brushstroke, reflecting the varied countries, cultures, and cuisines Thomas has experienced in his travels. Thomas envisions his restaurant as being much more than just a place to grab a bowl of chili; the eatery urges patrons to "think global and eat local."

Global Chili's menu features nearly every kind of chili under the sun, from gumbolike New Orleans style to Thai style with mangos and coconut milk. The Sedona chili blends chicken, sweet and russet potatoes, carrots, bacon, beans, and tomatoes with a plethora of spices and chile peppers. Thomas admits, "It takes some time, but so do most things worth doing."

Sedona Chili

1 teaspoon cayenne pepper

1 tablespoon ground cumin

1 teaspoon dried oregano

2 teaspoons paprika

1 1/3 pounds boneless chicken thighs, rinsed and diced

1 ancho chile

1 pasilla chile

1 dried New Mexico red chile

3 tablespoons light olive oil

2 chipotle peppers in adobo sauce

2/3 pound carrots, peeled and diced

1/3 pound russet potatoes, peeled and diced

1/3 pound sweet potatoes, peeled and diced

1 teaspoon salt

1/3 tablespoon freshly ground black pepper

1/4 pound cooked bacon, crumbled, 2 tablespoons fat reserved

2 cups chicken broth

1 1/3 cups diced yellow onions

2 tablespoons minced garlic

One 28-ounce can canned diced tomatoes with juice

1 cup cooked black beans, drained

1 cup canned white Northern beans

1 bottle Sam Adams beer

3 tablespoons packed brown sugar

2 cups water

2 1/2 cups fresh or frozen corn kernels

Chopped bell peppers and sour cream for garnish

Preheat the broiler. Mix the cayenne, cumin, oregano, and paprika together and place half in a self-sealing plastic bag; reserve the rest. Toss the chicken in the bag until coated. Refrigerate for at least 30 minutes. Toss the chiles in 1/2 tablespoon of the olive oil. Broil on a baking sheet, turning until they are puffed on all sides, about 5 minutes. Allow them to cool, and, using gloves, stem, seed, and tear them into pieces. Combine with the chipotle peppers, purée in a food processor, and set aside.

Preheat the oven to 375ºF. Toss the carrots and potatoes in 1 1/2 tablespoons of olive oil, salt, and pepper. Place on oiled baking sheets and roast until golden brown, about 1 hour, turning after 30 minutes. In a Dutch oven, cook the bacon and remove when browned. Then cook the chicken in the reserved bacon fat in batches. Discard the fat. Shred the chicken and set aside. Increase the heat to medium-high and add the remaining 1 tablespoon olive oil. Add the onions and garlic and cook for about 5 minutes. Add the tomatoes with juice, chili purée, beans, beer, sugar, and remaining spice mixture and cook for 20 minutes. Add the chicken broth and stir. Remove half the mixture from the Dutch oven and purée in a food processor with the water. Return the purée to the dutch oven. Add the reserved cooking liquid and simmer for 10 minutes. Stir in the corn and bake for 3 hours, checking every hour. Stir in the chicken and serve. *Serves 12 to 15.*

WESTERN U.S. ★ ★ KILLER CHILI

TAYLOR'S AUTOMATIC REFRESHER

SAN FRANCISCO, CALIFORNIA

Taylor's Automatic Refresher harkens back to the days of the American roadhouse, and while their food is comfortably old-fashioned, it's also undoubtedly modern. Fish and chips made with mahimahi, and heavenly espresso or white pistachio milkshakes complement their hamburgers—made from all-natural, grass-fed California Angus beef—and ahi tuna burgers with wasabi mayonnaise.

In 1999, brothers Joel and Duncan Gott renovated an old drive-in in St. Helena, California. The first location won acclaim from renowned wine critic Robert Parker, who declared the double cheeseburger his "most memorable meal of 1999." The second location, inside San Francisco's Ferry Building, opened in 2004.

A gigantic red neon sign demanding EAT hangs over the counter at the San Francisco spot—not that the diners really need the extra encouragement. This food, especially their chili, is the real San Francisco (and St. Helena) treat. Their seriously fantastic chili is warm, hearty, and packs a bit of a punch with beer—San Francisco's very own Anchor Steam.

Taylor's Automatic Refresher Chili

1 ½ pounds ground beef

1 yellow onion, diced

1 red bell pepper, seeded and diced

1 green bell pepper, seeded and diced

3 cloves garlic, minced

⅓ cup ground coriander

⅓ cup ground cumin

1 ½ cups (12 ounces) Anchor Steam beer

1 bay leaf

¾ cup (6 ounces) chipotle chiles in adobo sauce, puréed in a blender

⅓ cup chili powder

1 ½ cups (12 ounces) diced tomatoes

1 ½ cups (12 ounces) kidney beans, drained

Salt to taste

Shredded Cheddar cheese and chopped green onions, for garnish

In a large, heavy skillet, brown the beef over medium heat. Drain and discard all but 1 tablespoon of the fat. Transfer the meat to a bowl. In the same skillet, heat the reserved fat over medium heat and sauté the onion, peppers, and garlic until soft. Add the coriander, cumin, beer, and bay leaf and simmer for 3 minutes. Add the beef, puréed chipotle chiles, and chili powder. Add the tomatoes, beans, and salt. Reduce the heat to low and simmer for 45 minutes to 1 hour. Remove from the heat and let cool. Refrigerate overnight. Reheat. Remove the bay leaf. Serve the chili with the shredded cheese and onions. *Serves 4.*

WESTERN U.S. ★ ★ KILLER CHILI!

THE KITCHEN FOR EXPLORING FOODS

PASADENA, CALIFORNIA

For more than twenty years, Peggy Dark, owner of the Kitchen for Exploring Foods, has experimented with all sorts of flavors, textures, and ingredients that keep her customers begging for more. The Kitchen has received a Zagat Award of Distinction, and has been featured on *Today* and in *Gourmet* magazine. It's grown into one of the top catering companies in Los Angeles, and its Gourmet-To-Go location is Pasadena gourmands' idea of paradise. A large glass case is packed with salads, sandwiches, baked goods,

fresh fruit, and roasted veggies, and patrons can pick up boxed lunches to go. The demand for these boxed lunches, however, is so high that customers must order at least four days in advance.

Regular customers keep their fingers crossed on a daily basis that Dark and her staff will offer their White Chicken Chili. It's a creamy, utterly decadent chili that features navy beans, mild green chiles, chunks of chicken, Monterey jack cheese, and sour cream, and serving it with salsa adds the extra kick of fresh tomatoes.

White Chicken Chili

1 cup dried navy beans, picked over and rinsed

8 tablespoons (1 stick) unsalted butter

1 large onion, chopped

$1/4$ cup all-purpose flour

$3/4$ cup chicken broth

2 cups half-and-half

1 teaspoon Tabasco sauce, or to taste

$1^{1}/_{2}$ teaspoons chili powder

1 teaspoon ground cumin

$1/2$ teaspoon salt, or to taste

$1/2$ teaspoon freshly ground white pepper, or to taste

Two 4-ounce cans peeled whole green chiles, drained and chopped

5 boneless, skinless chicken breast halves, cooked and cut into $1/2$-inch pieces

$1^{1}/_{2}$ cups shredded Monterey jack cheese

$1/2$ cup sour cream

Fresh cilantro and salsa for garnish

In a medium pot, soak the beans overnight in enough cold water to cover the beans by 2 inches. Drain the beans in a colander and return to the pot with fresh cold water, covering the beans by 2 inches. Cook the beans at a bare simmer on very low heat until tender, about 1 hour, and drain in a colander.

In a medium skillet, melt 2 tablespoons of the butter over medium heat and cook the onion until softened. In a large, heavy pot, melt the remaining 6 tablespoons butter over medium-low heat and whisk in the flour to make a roux. Cook the roux, whisking constantly, for 3 minutes. Stir in the onion and gradually add the broth and half-and-half, whisking constantly. Bring the mixture to a boil, then reduce the heat to low and simmer, stirring occasionally, for 5 minutes or until thickened. Stir in the Tabasco, chili powder, cumin, salt, and white pepper. Add the beans, chiles, chicken, and cheese. Increase the heat to medium-low and cook, stirring frequently, for 20 minutes. Stir in the sour cream. Garnish with the cilantro and salsa. *Serves 4 to 6.*

TEAKWOODS BAR & GRILL

SCOTTSDALE, ARIZONA

If ever there were a quintessential neighborhood watering hole, then Teakwoods Bar & Grill is the place. The Scottsdale tavern prides itself on being a favorite spot of Scottsdale residents to eat, drink, chat, and catch a game on one of the bar's two dozen televisions. The beer selection is impressive, with a mix of stalwart favorites like Pabst Blue Ribbon and Guinness alongside smaller upstarts, such as Fat Tire from Colorado. Teakwoods even pours hometown brews like Kilt Lifter Scottish-Style Ale from Tempe, Arizona's Four Peaks Brewery.

Open for lunch and dinner (and, of course, happy hour), Teakwoods boasts a menu that ups the ante on pub grub. Diners can dig into fresh salads, five different kinds of hot dogs, lavosh, gyros, a slew of burgers and other sandwiches, and Uncle Tom's Moose Dip, which features sausage, black beans, cheese, and fresh jalapenos. Teakwoods also has a sumptuous chili on the menu, replete with tomatoes, onions, peppers, pinto and kidney beans, and ground beef. Made by chef Erik Olsen, this dish is best washed down with your favorite local beer.

Teakwoods Chili

Canola oil for sautéing

$\frac{1}{2}$ white onion, diced

1 red bell pepper, seeded and diced

1 green bell pepper, seeded and diced

1 $\frac{3}{4}$ pounds ground beef

76 $\frac{1}{2}$ ounces canned tomato strips

5 15-ounce cans tomato sauce

$\frac{1}{2}$ tablespoon freshly ground black pepper

$\frac{3}{4}$ teaspoon onion powder

2 tablespoons minced garlic

3/4 cup chili powder

$\frac{1}{4}$ tablespoon salt

Two 28-ounce cans kidney beans

Two 28-ounce cans pinto beans

In a large, heavy pot, heat the oil over medium heat and sauté the onion and bell peppers until the onion is translucent. Add the ground beef and cook until brown. Add the tomato strips, tomato sauce, black pepper, onion powder, garlic, chili powder, salt, and beans and mix thoroughly. Reduce the heat to low and simmer for 3 hours. Serve. *Serves 20.*

WILD BILL'S SALOON

BANFF, ALBERTA

Wild Bill's is aptly referred to as "Banff's legendary saloon." Its namesake was a real-life Western adventurer, but not the one you may be thinking of: Canada's version was named Wild Bill Peyto, not Cody. As the story goes, Peyto was born in England and immigrated to Canada in 1886. He settled in Banff and became a trail guide in the harsh Alberta wilderness, leading the very first group to climb Mt. Assiniboine. He later joined the Canadian Mounted Police, and is still considered to be one of western Canada's leading self-taught naturalists, hunters, geologists, and all-around outdoorsmen.

The eponymous Banff saloon is an homage not only to Wild Bill Peyto, but to Alberta's past and present cowboy ethos. Patrons can not only enjoy a good, hearty meal and a cold beer, but hear live bands, do the two-step in the dance hall, take in the majestic view on the patio, watch a football game, and even rope a calf. The décor is just as rugged as the terrain outdoors, with lots of wood, stone, and taxidermy. The food can best be described as Tex-Mex, and any such restaurant worth its salt has to have good chili. The smoky, zesty Wild Billy Chili is made with high-quality Alberta beef, two kinds of beans, chipotle chiles, dark beer, and tomatoes.

Wild Billy Chili

1½ pounds ground beef   + Pork or Bacon
¼ cup canola oil
3 onions, diced
1 green bell pepper, seeded and diced
1 red bell pepper, seeded and diced
¼ cup minced garlic
¼ cup red pepper flakes
¼ cup chili powder
2 tablespoons ground cumin
2 tablespoons ground coriander
1 tablespoon dried oregano, crumbled
1 cinnamon stick
½ can beer (the darker, the better)
1 tablespoon diced canned chipotle chiles
Four 14-ounce cans crushed tomatoes
One 14-ounce can red kidney beans
One 14-ounce can black beans
1 tablespoon liquid smoke
2 tablespoons Frank's RedHot Original Cayenne Pepper Sauce or other hot sauce
Salt and freshly ground black pepper to taste

Preheat the oven to 450°F. Put the ground beef in a large roasting pan and place in the oven. Bake, stirring occasionally to break up the meat, until the meat has started to brown, 20 to 40 minutes. Drain the cooked beef in a colander in the sink.

While the beef is cooking, in a large, heavy pot, heat the oil over medium-high heat. Add the onions and cook, stirring occasionally until they start to caramelize. Add the peppers and garlic and cook until soft. Add the spices, stir, and turn off the heat. Let sit for 5 to 10 minutes to release the flavor from the spices.

Return the pot to medium-high heat and add the beer, stirring to scrape up the browned bits from the bottom. Add all the remaining ingredients and the drained beef. Stir well and bring to a simmer, taking care not to burn the bottom. Simmer for 1 hour. Remove the cinnamon stick and add salt and pepper. *Serves 10 to 15.*

THE OLD COPPER KETTLE RESTAURANT & PUB

— FERGUS, ONTARIO —

If the thought of an old copper kettle conjures images of an English granny serving tea and cakes next to a crackling fire, your version is pretty close to the version in Fergus, Ontario. The Old Copper Kettle feels as cozy and comfortable as tea at your granny's might—if your granny also served nearly a dozen draft beers and hosted monthly Celtic and bluegrass jams.

The small town of Fergus is known for its annual summer truck show—reportedly the largest in North America—and for its Scottish Festival and Highland Games, where revelers don kilts, listen to pipe-and-drum music, and throw heavy stones and hammers. Located on St. Andrew Street, the town's primary thoroughfare, the Old Copper Kettle prides itself on being an authentic British Isles–style pub and a home away from

home for a strong expatriate contingent. The original pine floors and tin ceiling date back to the 1870s, and tea is served every afternoon. The menu, which exclusively features homemade dishes crafted from local ingredients, includes typical pub fare, such as bangers and mash, shepherd's pie, and Cornish pasties, along with sandwiches, salads, and soups.

Chili may seem an odd choice for a British pub in Canada, but it fits well with the stick-to-your-ribs traditional U.K. dishes. This recipe is simple, with a relatively short list of ingredients, but a creamy, country-style ale gives the chili a depth of flavor and is perfect for serving alongside it. The Old Copper Kettle uses an ale from Wellington Brewery in neighboring Guelph, Ontario, but any malty, full-bodied ale will work in its place.

Wellington County Pub Chili

4 tablespoons canola oil

2 onions, chopped

5 tablespoons chili powder

3 garlic cloves, minced

2 tablespoons tomato purée

2 pounds ground beef

1 bay leaf

One 28-ounce can tomatoes

2 cups Wellington County Ale or other malty ale

One 28-ounce can kidney beans, drained

Shredded aged Cheddar cheese for garnish

In a large, heavy pot, heat 1 tablespoon of the oil over medium heat and sauté the onions until soft. Add the chili powder, garlic, tomato purée, the remaining 3 table-spoons oil, and the ground beef in small batches, browning and stirring it in with the onions and spice. Add the bay leaf and tomatoes. Add the ale and simmer for 1 hour. Add the kidney beans and simmer for 15 minutes. Remove the bay leaf. Serve in individual bowls. Top with shredded aged Cheddar cheese. *Serves 6 to 8.*

GENERAL COOKIN' TIP

★ As with most chili, this is best cooked the day before and then reheated.

THE DISH & THE RUNAWAY SPOON

EDMONTON, ALBERTA

Life is full of mysteries worth pondering: Is there life on Mars? How does Donald Trump get his hair to do that? And whatever happened to the dish and the spoon after they ditched that cat and fiddle and ran away together? We may never know the answers to those other burning questions, but it appears that the nursery-rhyme tableware relocated to Canada.

Fans of Edmonton's favorite bistro, the Dish (and its sister catering company, the Runaway Spoon), use words such as "funky," "eclectic," and "quirky" to describe the atmosphere of the place. Owner Carole Amerongen and her crew, not surprisingly, take old favorites and re-imagine them in fresh, inventive ways. Menu offerings include Parmesan and spinach risotto cakes, a mango-curry chicken wrap, a deep-dish sweet potato shepherd's pie, and a rustic lamb stew. Even their chili is perked up, as they've substituted bison for standard beef or pork, and added three types of beans, herbed tomato sauce, and a slew of veggies and spices. It's so good, you'll be over the moon, too.

The Dish Bison Chili

1 cup dried pinto beans

1 cup dried black beans

Canola oil for sautéing

2 cups sliced onions

$\frac{1}{2}$ tablespoon minced garlic

1 cup diced green bell peppers

5 ounces button mushrooms, sliced

$1\frac{1}{4}$ pounds ground bison

$\frac{1}{2}$ cup fresh or frozen corn kernels

$2\frac{1}{4}$ cups tomato sauce with basil and oregano

Two 28-ounce cans chopped tomatoes

10 ounces canned kidney beans, drained

$\frac{3}{4}$ teaspoon red pepper flakes

2 tablespoons chili powder

1 tablespoon ground cumin

$\frac{1}{2}$ tablespoon ground coriander

$\frac{3}{4}$ tablespoon minced chipotle chiles in adobo sauce (add more for a spicier chili)

$\frac{1}{2}$ tablespoon salt

$\frac{1}{2}$ tablespoon freshly ground pepper

$1\frac{1}{2}$ tablespoons fresh lime juice

2 tablespoons packed brown sugar

Shredded Cheddar cheese, sour cream, and fresh cilantro for garnish

Pick over and rinse the beans. In a large saucepan, soak the beans overnight in water to cover by 2 inches.

In a large, heavy pot, heat the oil over medium heat and sauté the onions, garlic, peppers, and mushrooms until the onions are translucent. Add the ground bison and brown. Add the corn, tomato sauce, and tomatoes. Cook for 1 hour. Add the spices, salt, pepper, lime juice, and sugar, reduce the heat to low, and simmer for 1 hour. Drain the soaked beans and add to the pot along with the kidney beans. Cook for 1 hour. Garnish with Cheddar cheese, a dollop of sour cream, and cilantro and serve. *Serves 8.*

THE BOILER HOUSE RESTAURANT

TORONTO, ONTARIO

If you're a fan of industrial-chic design and wildly innovative cuisine, then Toronto's Boiler House is for you. Located in an old two-story warehouse in the hip, historic Distillery District, the chophouse features a twenty-two-foot-long wine rack, hardwood floors, and hand-carved timber tables. Coveys of smaller, more intimate dining spaces dot the open space.

The Boiler House has garnered awards since its inception, due in no small part to the masterful styling of executive chef Jason Rosso. *USA Today* praised the restaurant's "big-city sophistication [and] small-town charm." The Boiler House's dishes, which include an East Coast cod and green onion cake with sour-pickle relish and citrus butter, and a grilled bone-in New York strip steak with vanilla-scented sweet potatoes and goat cheese–sage glacé, push the culinary envelope; it's steak and seafood dressed to the nines.

Rosso first made his adventurous lobster chili at Peller Estates Winery in Ontario's Niagara region, and even graciously shared his recipe with Canada's Food Network. It's lobster and chili unlike you've ever tasted them before: together. For this dish, Rosso makes his own homemade chili powder, which you can keep to use in other recipes. Pair this chili with a bottle of semi-dry Riesling, a Sauvignon Blanc, or a Gewürztraminer for a truly decadent dinner.

Lobster Chili

Homemade Chili Powder

    6 tablespoons paprika

    2 tablespoons ground turmeric

    1 tablespoon red pepper flakes

    1 teaspoon ground cumin

    1 teaspoon dried oregano, crumbled

    $\frac{1}{2}$ teaspoon cayenne pepper

    $\frac{1}{2}$ teaspoon garlic powder

    $\frac{1}{2}$ teaspoon salt

    $\frac{1}{4}$ teaspoon ground cloves

1 tablespoon olive oil

3 shallots, minced

2 cloves garlic, minced

2 stalks celery, finely chopped

1 yellow bell pepper, seeded and finely chopped

One 15-ounce can kidney beans, drained

$\frac{1}{4}$ cup tomato paste

1 cup fish or lobster stock, or as desired

Two $1\frac{1}{4}$-pound lobsters, cooked, shelled, and diced

$\frac{1}{2}$ cup heavy cream

For the chili powder: Combine all the spices in a coffee or spice grinder and blend to a fine powder. You will not need all of the chili powder, but it keeps very well in a jar for another use.

In a heavy, medium pot, heat the olive oil over medium heat. Add the shallots, garlic, celery, and yellow pepper and sauté for 6 minutes. Add the kidney beans, 3 tablespoons of the chili powder, and the tomato paste and cook for 5 minutes, stirring constantly. The mixture will seem very thick, so add the stock to thin it out to your desired consistency. (You may need to add a little water to thin it down, as well.) Cook the chili base for 10 minutes, stirring constantly. Add the diced lobster meat and cream. Cook for about 1 minute, or until the lobster is heated through. Taste and adjust the seasoning. *Serves 6.*

MUDDY WATERS SMOKEHOUSE & BLUES

WINNIPEG, MANITOBA

Muddy Waters Smokehouse & Blues touts itself as "the place that loves to party," and you have to trust that a restaurant that encourages its guests to sign their names on its walls means business. Besides that, it may well be the closest thing to the Deep South in Canada. Located in Winnipeg's the Forks market, Muddy Waters serves up both authentic and admittedly "not-so-authentic" Southern favorites and hospitality.

As the name implies, ribs are the main event here. Manitobans can feast on all things ribs to their hearts'

content: fried rib tips, pulled rib meat nachos, a smoked rib meat sandwich, and barbecued chicken and rib combo platters. One of the few non-rib items on the menu is the Muddy Waters Chili, which combines ground beef, tomatoes, kidney beans, and a sharp, tasty blend of spices. The real kicker comes at the end, when the entire concoction is poured into a casserole dish, layered with shredded Monterey jack or Cheddar cheese and baked for a few minutes in the oven. The result is a gooey, cheesy delight sure to fill you up.

Muddy Waters Chili

1 tablespoon canola oil
1 pound ground beef
1 green bell pepper, seeded and diced
1 yellow onion, diced
2 stalks celery, diced
1 jalapeno chile, minced
2 cloves garlic, minced
$1/2$ teaspoon ground cumin
2 teaspoons chili powder
$1/2$ teaspoon cayenne pepper
1 tablespoon packed brown sugar
$1/2$ teaspoon dry mustard
16 ounces canned kidney beans, drained
16 ounces crushed tomatoes
2 plum (Roma) tomatoes, diced
Salt and freshly ground pepper to taste
$1/2$ cup shredded Monterey jack or Cheddar cheese
Snipped fresh chives for garnish

Preheat the oven to 375°F. In a large, heavy skillet heat the oil over medium heat and brown the beef. Add the green pepper, onion, celery, jalapeno, and garlic and sauté until slightly tender. Mix all the dry ingredients together in a separate bowl. Add to the beef mixture and stir thoroughly to avoid lumps. Cook until the vegetables are tender, about 10 minutes. Add the kidney beans, crushed tomatoes, diced tomatoes, and salt and pepper and bring to a boil. Reduce the heat to low and simmer for 1 hour, stirring occasionally. Place in a casserole dish, top with the cheese, and bake for 5 to 6 minutes, or until the cheese is melted. Garnish with the chives and serve. *Serves 4 to 6.*

THE SHERWOOD HOUSE RESTAURANT

CANMORE, ALBERTA

If your idea of perfection includes mountain vistas, roaring fireplaces, and log cabins, you need look no further than Canmore, Alberta. Situated in the Canadian Rockies, the area is a tourist hotspot, well known for its glorious skiing and snowboarding, hiking, rock-climbing (and even dog-sledding), and its postcard-perfect scenic beauty.

After a long day navigating the slopes or gallivanting across mountainous terrain, visitors can relax and refuel at the Sherwood House Restaurant, which looks and feels like a big, cozy log cabin, complete with the requisite stone fireplace and wood, wood everywhere. Guests have been visiting this alpine retreat for nearly a century to dine on authentic Canadian cuisine, hear live music, and warm up with a drink at the bar. The menu is game-heavy: venison, ostrich, and bison feature prominently alongside rainbow trout and Alberta beef. Chili is a must for its substance and heat, but the Sherwood House's variety does things a little differently. This chili recipe combines the traditional ground beef, kidney beans, and spices with chorizo sausage, sun-dried tomatoes, and potato for a unique flavor and texture.

Sun-Dried Tomato & Sausage Chili

2 tablespoons olive oil

1 red onion, diced

1$\frac{1}{2}$ pounds ground beef

11 ounces chorizo sausage, chopped

4 tomatoes, diced

$\frac{1}{4}$ cup oil-packed sun-dried tomatoes, drained and chopped

1 russet potato, peeled and diced

One 6-ounce can tomato paste

One 6-ounce can kidney beans, drained

1 garlic clove, minced

3 tablespoons chili powder

$\frac{1}{4}$ teaspoon red pepper flakes, or to taste

1 teaspoon packed brown sugar

1 tablespoon dried oregano, crumbled

1 tablespoon ground cumin

1 cup water

Salt and freshly ground black pepper to taste

In a large, heavy pot, heat the oil over medium heat and sauté the onion. Add the beef and sausage and brown. Add all the remaining ingredients and reduce the heat to medium-low. Cover and simmer for 1$\frac{1}{2}$ hours. Season with salt and pepper. *Serves 6.*

GENERAL COOKIN' TIP

★ Instead of the red pepper flakes, you can substitute minced green chile, such as jalapeno or serrano.

M<small>c</small>SORLEY'S SALOON & GRILL

— TORONTO, ONTARIO —

McSorley's Saloon & Grill is one of those places that doesn't take itself too seriously, from the beer and hockey paraphernalia covering nearly every free centimeter of wall space, to the contents of its menu. Vegetarian dishes are marked with the McSorley's take on the iconic no-smoking symbol—a bone in a circle with a slash through it—and many of the dishes have wacky names: Take the All-Day Hangover Breakfast or the Kabob's Your Uncle, for instance. The best part is that the food doesn't just have a sense of humor, it tastes great, too. While much of it is standard bar-and-grill fare, the McSorley's menu includes some unexpectedly transcontinental items, such as pad Thai, pot stickers, and samosas.

McSorley's gives bar chili a good (and healthy) makeover, as well. Its vegetarian chili is a veritable garden patch of veggies: corn, onion, sweet peppers, tomatoes, beans, garlic, celery, chickpeas, and fresh cilantro, with the surprise kick of fresh ginger. It's served with nacho chips, and owner Simon Hamlon swears it's the best veggie chili ever made. So good, in fact, that you'll make no bones about forgetting its meat-free designation.

McSorley's Wonderful Veggie Chili

Olive oil for sautéing

2 large carrots, peeled and chopped

1 large white onion, chopped

2 stalks celery, chopped

1 red bell pepper, seeded and chopped

1 green bell pepper, seeded and chopped

1 clove garlic, minced

1½-inch piece fresh ginger, minced

2 bay leaves

1 teaspoon dried thyme

1 teaspoon dried rosemary

1 teaspoon cayenne pepper

2 tablespoons chili powder

One 28-ounce can plum tomatoes

One 19-ounce can kidney beans, drained

One 19-ounce can chickpeas (garbanzo beans), drained

One 5½-ounce can tomato paste

2 cups frozen corn kernels

½ cup chopped fresh cilantro

2 dashes Frank's RedHot Sauce or other hot sauce

In a large, heavy saucepan, heat the oil over medium heat and sauté the carrots, onion, celery, peppers, garlic, and ginger for 10 minutes. Add the bay leaves, thyme, rosemary, cayenne, and chili powder. Add the tomatoes, beans, chickpeas, tomato paste, and corn and simmer for 20 minutes. Remove the bay leaves. Add the cilantro and hot sauce. Serve. *Serves 4.*

OH! CANADA

CALGARY, ALBERTA

Like its neighbor to the south, Canada is a melting pot of diverse people from all corners of the globe speaking different languages, practicing different customs, and eating different foods. Canadian cuisine, though certainly influenced by English and French culinary traditions, is equally influenced by other European, Asian, African, and Latin foods. That said, Canadians are certainly proud of their own culinary heritage. Oh! Canada Restaurant & Bar wears that pride on its sleeve (or, at least, on its sign). Located in the Nexen Tower in downtown Calgary, Oh! Canada specializes in Canadian cuisine. The menu, with dishes

prepared by Oh! Canada's "kitchen prime minister," Scott Sprouse, features such enticing edibles as a Green Party salad, the Gretzky smoked-turkey sandwich, the Tragically Hip Alberta beef sandwich, and Newfie Fish & Chips.

Oh! Canada also serves some remarkable chili. While it doesn't have a funky name or feature distinctly Canadian ingredients, it is its own melting pot of flavors and spices. Want to "eat, drink, and be Canadian," as Oh! Canada's motto urges? Serve this chili while watching your favorite hockey team on the tube or after a day on the ice.

Oh! Canada Chili

3 pounds ground beef sirloin

2 tablespoons extra-virgin olive oil

2 large yellow onions, finely chopped

10 garlic cloves, minced

2 cups fresh or frozen corn kernels

1/4 cup red pepper flakes

2 tablespoons ground cumin

1 tablespoon chili powder

16 ounces canned kidney beans, drained and rinsed

16 ounces canned chickpeas (garbanzo beans), drained and rinsed

16 ounces canned whole tomatoes with juice

16 ounces canned tomato purée

1/2 cup warm water

1 teaspoon seasoned salt (preferably Lawry's)

1 tablespoon freshly ground black pepper

Shredded aged Cheddar cheese and sliced green onions for garnish

In a large, heavy skillet, heat the olive oil over medium heat and brown the beef. Drain the fat and reserve the meat.

In a clean large, heavy skillet, heat the remaining 1 tablespoon of olive oil over medium-high heat and cook the onions and garlic until the onions are translucent. Add the corn, cooked sirloin, and all of the seasonings. Give it a quick stir and add the beans, whole tomatoes with juice, and tomato purée. Reduce the heat to medium-low and simmer for 2 hours, adjusting the consistency with the water. Season with the salt and pepper. Garnish with the shredded Cheddar and green onions and serve with corn bread, if desired. *Serves 6 to 8.*

THE STILL BAR & GRILL

KITCHENER, ONTARIO

One-half of Ontario's Twin Cities, Kitchener boasts at least one thing that its sister city, Waterloo, doesn't have: the Still Bar & Grill. And what does the Still have that other bar-grill establishments in the area don't have? The largest patio in the bi-city area, its own nightclub, and an outdoor beach volleyball court, for starters.

With so much going on under one roof, you might assume that the food would be an afterthought, a mere edible napkin of sorts to soak up the Tequila Poppers and Cowboy Cocktails, but you would be wrong. It's not health food, but it's good food. Of particular note is the Still Chili, which gets extra-special attention on Cowboy Thursdays, when Twin City urban cowboys (and girls) come out to eat, drink, and be merry. Try whipping this chili up the next time a herd of friends moseys on over to your place; it's super quick, super easy, and super tasty. It can be thrown together on a whim too, as you probably already have all the ingredients, and the dish takes only a few minutes to cook.

The Still Chili

1 large onion, diced

1 large red bell pepper, seeded and diced

1 large green bell pepper, seeded and diced

11 pounds lean ground beef

12 cups chili sauce

12 cups tomato-based pasta sauce

12 cups cooked kidney beans

$1/2$ beef bouillon cube dissolved in $1/2$ cup water

Cayenne pepper, to taste

In a large, heavy pot, combine the onion, peppers, and ground beef and brown over medium-high heat. Add the sauces, kidney beans, dissolved bouillon cube, and cayenne and stir to combine. Simmer for 10 minutes, then serve. *Serves 15.*

GENERAL COOKIN' TIP

★ The dissolved bouillon cube can be replaced with $1/2$ cup beef broth.

TOMATO FRESH FOOD CAFÉ

VANCOUVER, BRITISH COLUMBIA

"Fresh" has become such a buzzword in the restaurant world that it barely manages to catch diners' eyes anymore. In Vancouver, lovers of good food have the good fortune of the Tomato Fresh Food Café, where "fresh food" isn't just a catchphrase, but a mission. Owner James Gaudreault, along with his wife, Star Spilos, and chef James Campbell, opened the café in the early '90s with the intention of creating a cozy, comfortable, and affordable place where people could enjoy fresh, delicious, innovative meals made from local and mostly organic ingredients. Sound simple? It is, and that's exactly the point—it's a fuss- and fad-free approach to food. Vancouver residents have taken notice, and the Tomato Fresh Food Café is now a favorite fixture on Cambie Street. Many patrons frequent the bright, cheery café several times a week, and *Vancouver* magazine voted it the Best Neighbourhood Restaurant in 2003. Gaudreault and Spilos even penned their own cookbook of recipes from the restaurant, called *As Fresh as It Gets*, in 2006.

Tomato Fresh Food Café Vegetarian Chili

¹/₄ cup plus 6 tablespoons olive oil

1 unpeeled eggplant, cut into ¹/₂-inch dice

2 onions, finely diced

4 garlic cloves, minced

1 jalapeno chile, minced

1 cup button mushrooms, quartered

2 small green bell peppers, seeded and finely diced

1 cup V-8 vegetable juice

One 28-ounce can chopped plum tomatoes

2 cups finely diced fresh plum tomatoes

2 tablespoons ground ancho chile

1 tablespoons ground cumin

1 teaspoons ground fennel

1 tablespoon freshly ground black pepper

1 tablespoon salt

1 cup canned dark red kidney beans, drained and rinsed

1 cup canned garbanzo beans (chickpeas), drained and rinsed

¹/₂ cup fresh dill, chopped

¹/₂ cup fresh Italian flat-leaf parsley, chopped

1 tablespoon fresh oregano, chopped

1 tablespoon fresh basil, chopped

2 tablespoons fresh lemon juice

1 cup shredded Cheddar or Monterey jack cheese

In a large skillet, heat the ¹/₄ cup olive oil over medium heat. Add the eggplant and sauté until almost tender. Using a slotted spoon, transfer to a large bowl. In the same skillet, heat the 6 tablespoons olive oil over low heat. Add the onions, garlic, jalapeno, mushrooms, and bell peppers. Sauté until softened, about 10 minutes. Add the sautéed eggplant, V-8 juice, canned and fresh plum tomatoes, ground ancho chile, cumin, fennel, black pepper, and salt. Cook, uncovered, stirring ocasionally, for 30 minutes. Add the kidney and garbanzo beans, dill, parsley, oregano, basil, and lemon juice. Cook for another 15 minutes. Stir well, taste, and adjust the seasonings. Serve topped with the shredded Cheddar or Monterey jack cheese. *Serves 8 to 10.*

INDEX

ACKNOWLEDGMENTS

Thanks to all the chefs and restaurant owners who generously shared their chili recipes, photographs, and stories to make this book possible.

Thanks and love to Scott, the Andersons, the Witmers, and all of my family and friends. Thanks also to the faculty, administration, staff, and students at Shippensburg University.

Thanks to everyone at becker&mayer! Extra-special thanks to Kate Perry, Kasey Free, Lisa Metzger, Shirley Woo, and Kjersti Egerdahl.

Thanks to everyone at Chronicle Books.

RESOURCES

Chili Appreciation Society International, International Chili Society, The Food Network, Jane & Michael Stern, *Gourmet*, *Bon Appetit*, Epicurious.com, and National Public Radio.

IMAGE CREDITS

All interior photographs are courtesy of each respective restaurant, except for the following: page 6 (right): Saint Louis Zoo; page 7 (center image): © becker&mayer!; page 14: Jim MacNeill; page 26: Luke Nerone/Juke Photographers; page 44: Saint Louis Zoo; page 54: © becker&mayer!; page 58: © becker&mayer!; page 64: © becker&mayer!; page 66: © becker&mayer!; page 76: Jocelyn Barda; page 84: © becker&mayer!; page 86: © becker&mayer!

If any unintended omissions have been made, becker&mayer! would be pleased to add appropriate acknowledgements in future editions.